A KALEIDOSCOPE KIDS® BOOK

W9-AUR-879

Lighthouses
of North America!

**Exploring Their
* History, Lore & Science ***

Lisa Trumbauer

Illustrations by
Michael Kline

WILLIAMSON BOOKS • NASHVILLE, TENNESSEE

Dedication

For Dave, as always. LT

═══════

Photographs: cover: Bodie Island Light, U.S. Coast Guard; **p. 7:** Boston Light © SuperStock Inc./SuperStock; **p. 13:** Cape Disappointment Lighthouse, U.S. Coast Guard; **p. 16:** Sandy Hook Light © Sydney Wright; **p. 22:** Portland Head Light © Bob & Sandra Shanklin, The Lighthouse People, www.thelighthousepeople.com; **p. 26:** Makapuu Point Light, National Park Service/photograph by James P. Delgado; **p. 35:** Michigan Island Light, © Bob & Sandra Shanklin, The Lighthouse People, www.thelighthousepeople.com; **p. 37:** Bodie Island Light, © Ann Shelton, Keep the Lights Shining, www.angelfire.com/va3/keepthelightsshining/index.html; **p. 38:** Point Vicente Light, U.S. Coast Guard; **p. 44:** Ponce de Leon Inlet Light © Ponce de Leon Inlet Lighthouse Preservation Association, www.ponceinlet.org; **p. 51:** Cape Hinchinbrook, © Bob & Sandra Shanklin, The Lighthouse People, www.thelighthousepeople.com; **p. 53:** Minots Ledge Light, U.S. Coast Guard; **p. 56:** Sambro Island Lighthouse © Chris Mills, Pharos Communications, www.ns.sympatico.ca/ketm; **p. 61:** Thomas Point Shoal Light © Henry Gonzalez, U.S. Lighthouse Society, www.uslhs.org; **p. 65:** Duxbury Pier Lighthouse © Project Gurnet and Bug Lights, Inc., www.buglight.org; **p. 70:** East Brother Island Lighthouse, © East Brother Light Station, www.ebls.org; **p. 75:** Ida Lewis, U.S. Coast Guard; **p. 87:** Sally Snowman, courtesy of Sally Snowman; **p. 88:** Holland Harbor Light © Ann Shelton, Keep the Lights Shining, www.angelfire.com/va3/keepthelightsshining/index.html; **p. 89:** Chatham Light © Chatham Historical Society, www.chathamhistoricalsociety.org/; The Beacon Restaurant © Skippy Sanchez

Acknowledgments: p. 7: Boston Light Bill, www.lighthouse.cc/boston/history.html; **p. 8:** Statement of R.A. Allen, third officer of the *Anglo-Saxon* in *Newfoundland Express*, *May 5, 1863*, www.theshipslist.com/ships/Wrecks/anglosaxon.htm; **p. 11:** "Minots Ledge" by Fitz James O'Brien, www.cdl.library.cornell.edu/moa/images/bibcite.gif; **p. 21:** "The Lighthouse" by Henry Wadsworth Longfellow, www.hwlongfellow.org; "Lighthouse, Oh Lighthouse" by Nicolette Basiliere and Andrea Racine is used by permission; **p. 44:** "The Open Boat" by Stephen Crane, www.ponceinlet.org/historystephencrane.html; **p. 47:** *A History of Lighthouses* by Patrick Beaver, published by Peter Davies, London: 1971; **p. 63:** annual report of U.S. Lighthouse Board, 1873, www.thomaspointlighthouse.org/annualReports.asp; **p. 65:** *Bug Light* by Harry Salter, www.lighthouse.cc/duxbury/history.html; **p. 68:** St. George Reef Light, Historical Information at U.S. Coast Guard Historic Light Information, www.uscg.mil/hq/gcp/history/WEBLIGHTHOUSES/LHCA.html; **p. 72:** "Lighthouse Keepers," www.home.comcast.net/~debee2/NNNS/KeepersPoem.html, as told by Captain Stetson Turner to the staff of the Shore Village Museum (Maine's Lighthouse Museum) www.mainelighthousemuseum.com/; **p. 74:** Instructions for Keepers of Lighthouses within the United States, the U.S. Lighthouse Board; www.cr.nps.gov/maritime/keep/keep19th.htm; **p. 76:** Elizabeth Williams quote, *Women Who Kept the Lights* by Mary Louise Clifford and J. Candace Clifford, © 1993 and 2001 by Cypress Communications, Alexandria, VA: 2000; **p. 78:** Annie Bell Hobbs quote, *Women Who Kept the Lights* by Mary Louise Clifford and J. Candace Clifford; Cypress Communications, Alexandria, VA: 2000; **p. 81:** letter by Abbie Burgess, *Women Who Kept the Lights* by Mary Louise Clifford and J. Candace Clifford; Cypress Communications, Alexandria, VA: 2000 and www.lighthouse.cc/matinicusrock/history.html; **p. 82:** Edward Rowe Snow, www.lighthouse.cc/saddleback/history.html; June Dudley Watts as told to Cheryl Shelton-Roberts, co-author (with Bruce Roberts) of *Lighthouse Families*, www.lighthouse.cc/saddleback/history.html; **p. 84:** from a newspaper article recounting how keeper Margaret Novell helped during a storm, *Women Who Kept the Lights* by Mary Louise Clifford and J. Candace Clifford, Cypress Communications, Alexandria, VA: 2000. **p. 89:** Keeper Oswald Allik's final entry in the station log, preserved at the Columbia River Maritime Museum in Astoria, www.pbs.org/legendarylighthouses/html/pnworgl.html#tillamook

Text copyright © 2007 by Lisa Trumbauer
Illustrations copyright © 2007 by Michael Kline
All rights reserved. No portion of this book may be reproduced mechanically, electronically, or by any other means including photocopying or on the Internet without written permission of the publisher.

Library of Congress Cataloging-in-Publication Data
Trumbauer, Lisa, 1963-
  Lighthouses of North America! : exploring their history, lore & science /
Lisa Trumbauer ; Illustrations by Michael Kline.
      p. cm. – (Kaleidoscope kids)
   Includes index.
   ISBN-13: 978-0-8249-6790-1 (pbk. : alk. paper)
   ISBN-13: 978-0-8249-6791-8 (case : alk. paper)
   ISBN-10: 0-8249-6790-9 (pbk. : alk. paper)
   ISBN-10: 0-8249-6791-7 (case : alk. paper)
   1. Lighthouses–North America–Juvenile literature. 2. Early childhood education–Activity programs–Juvenile literature. I. Kline, Michael P. II.
Title.
   VK1022.T89 2007
   387.1'550973--dc22
                              2006036188

Kaleidoscope Kids® series editor: **Susan Williamson**

Project editor: **Vicky Congdon**
Interior design: **Sydney Wright**
Illustrations: **Michael Kline**
Cover design and illustration: **Michael Kline**

Published by Williamsonbooks
An imprint of Ideals Publications
A Guideposts Company
535 Metroplex Drive, Suite 250
Nashville, Tennessee 37211
www.idealsbooks.com
800-586-2572

Printed and bound in Singapore

10 9 8 7 6 5 4 3 2 1

Kids Can!®, *Little Hands*®, *Quick Starts for Kids!*®, *Kaleidoscope Kids*®, and *Tales Alive!*® are registered trademarks of Ideals Publications, a Guideposts Company.

Good Times Books™, *Little Hands Story Corners*™, and *Quick Starts Tips!*™ are trademarks of Ideals Publications, a Guideposts Company.

Notice: The information contained in this book is true, complete, and accurate to the best of our knowledge. All recommendations and suggestions are made without any guarantees on the part of the author or Ideals Publications. The author and publisher disclaim all liability incurred in conjunction with the use of this information.

Contents

Lighthouses!
North America's Lifesavers

Which buildings in North America — and around the world — have been responsible for saving hundreds, even thousands, of lives? Lighthouses!

Lighthouses are among the oldest structures built in the United States and Canada. From tall, conical towers to squatty coffeepot–shaped "bugs," lighthouses have lit up North America's shores for centuries. They've guided ships along the Atlantic Coast, the Pacific Coast, the Gulf Coast, and the coasts of the Great Lakes, saving the lives of people traveling by ship. Lighthouses are marvels of construction and an enduring reflection of North America's past.

In this book, you'll explore why lighthouses were so necessary to the settlement of the United States and Canada. You'll discover the dangers that lie hidden beneath the waves, and you'll hear from shipwreck survivors how lighthouses and their keepers saved their lives. You'll also meet the extraordinary people who worked and lived at lighthouses, and you'll experience what living in a lighthouse was like, for adults *and* kids.

A lighthouse might seem like a simple structure, but building one was anything but easy. Whether lighthouses were built on rocky land, shifting sand, or even in the middle of an island or the water, their construction was a tremendous feat and took enormous effort. And don't forget that all-important light! Candles, reflectors, prisms, and the modern lightbulb all played a part in the history — and science — of the lighthouse. We'll take a look inside the lighthouse to see just what makes it operational and how it is able to shine for miles (km) out to sea, preventing countless catastrophes and loss of life.

So get ready for an amazing journey involving science, history — and even a bit of legend and ghostly mystery! — as we explore the lighthouses of North America.

Lisa Trumbauer

Lisa Trumbauer

CHAPTER 1

A Matter of Light — or Death!

* Why Lighthouses Were Built *

Captain's Log
February 15, 1863
Portland, Maine

We have made it safely to the New England coast, but no less than twelve hours ago I doubted the survival of not only myself and my crew, but my ship and its cargo as well.

We were but a few miles offshore when, without warning, a huge storm was upon us. The sky and the seas turned black, and heavy sheets of rain pounded against the deck and the sails. A tremendous wind accompanied the foul weather. Night fell fast, and we soon lost all sight of the coastline. The ship rocked and rolled perilously beneath our feet, and I thought for certain that we were all doomed.

Then, to our great relief, a steady, strong light appeared in the distance. The beacon glowed more brightly, the closer we drew to it. Through the rain we could eventually make out the tall tower. The lighthouse was a most welcome sight, and it truly saved our lives this night.

—Captain David Smythe

oday, many lighthouses seem like nothing more than cool-looking buildings that dot the shore. For more than 200 years, however, it was a different story along the coastlines of North America. Mariners — sailors, fisherman, and others who traveled on the water in all kinds of weather — relied upon them in order to make it safely to land. The beam of a lighthouse was often the only thing that saved these navigators from treacherous waters — pounding surf, rocky shores, or hidden shallow spots where ships could run aground. These sturdy beacons were a matter of life or death!

Let's dig into a little coastal geology to see why and where these lifesaving structures were built.

Challenging Coastlines

For hundreds of years, the most efficient means of traveling long distances was by boat. Sometimes, as in the case of traveling from Europe to America, it was the only way to go! Making sure ships reached their destinations was not only a matter of keeping passengers safe, it was necessary for trade as well.

Take a look at the maps of the United States and Canada on pages 90 to 91, as well as the smaller regional U.S. maps on pages 11 and 60. Are the coastlines smooth and solid? Are they one gently curving line? Definitely not!

In many places, the east and west coasts of this continent are craggy and broken, full of wide bays and narrow inlets, jutting points of land, and rocky shorelines that can all be difficult to navigate. Even smooth sandy coastlines have their challenges (see page 12). What's more, many port cities are located within protected coves or bays, away from the main coastline. Entering these harbors in the dark was not an easy feat! As you look at these maps, think about how guiding lights would be helpful in these different locations.

Busy Harbors

When Europeans first began arriving on the shores of North America, no lighthouses lit up the shores. As an ever-increasing number of ships began sailing to this "new world," this became quite a problem. One of the busiest harbors in America was Boston. In 1715, the Boston Light Bill (see section at right), explaining the need for a lighthouse at Boston Harbor to ensure that trade ships could get in and out safely, was passed, and America's first lighthouse was in the works! (The document refers to "his majesty's subjects" because in 1715, the colonies were still under the rule of King George back in England.)

Whereas the want [lack] of a lighthouse erected at the entrance to the harbor of Boston hath been a great discouragement to navigation by the loss of the lives and estates of several of his majesty's subjects; for prevention thereof—Be it enacted … that there be a lighthouse erected at the charge of the Province, on the southernmost part of the Great Brewster [Island] … to be kept lighted from sun setting to sun rising.

Still Lighting the Way!

Boston Light, Massachusetts — America's First Lighthouse!

Built in 1716, Boston Light marks the entrance to Boston Harbor. The original stone tower stood about 70 feet (21.5 m) tall.

The lighthouse that stands today is not the original lighthouse. During the American Revolution, the Boston Light became a target. In 1775, the British controlled Boston Harbor. The colonists figured that destroying the lighthouse would hinder the British. So that July, colonial soldiers sneaked onto the island and burned the lighthouse's wooden parts. One year later, the British had their turn; they blew up the lighthouse, completely demolishing it. Reconstruction began as the Revolutionary War was drawing to a close in 1783, and that's the lighthouse that's still in operation today.

Cliff Ahoy!

Along some coastlines, there aren't any gently sloping sandy beaches or welcoming harbors where the sea meets the land. Instead, the shoreline ends abruptly at a steep cliff that drops straight down to the ocean. Many lighthouses were built on cliffs such as these to alert boats that they were approaching a wall of rock. After all, in the dark, it can be impossible to determine whether you're approaching a dark stretch of open water — or a large mountain of land.

One such dangerous spot in northeastern Canada is Cape Race off the island of Newfoundland. In 1863, a passenger ship called the *Anglo-Saxon* crashed into the cliffs as it tried to navigate through thick fog and heavy ice — even though a lighthouse was there! Nearly 300 people died, but miraculously, about 130 people were rescued by the lighthouse keeper (for more on these courageous folks, see pages 71–84), and others were picked up by steamships in the area.

"When I got into the water I struck out for the raft, and I got on it … Captain Hyler and myself hauled the ship's cook and the boy on the raft … We now cut the raft clear of the wreck, and it floated away. … We drifted about all night, and soon after sunrise saw the steamer, but … despaired of being seen; I got a staff, and hoisted a woman's dress upon it. They saw the signal, and came down and picked us up."

—Mr. R. A. Allen, third officer of the *Anglo-Saxon*, rescued by the steamer *Dauntless*

Light up a steep cliff

What you need
- ⚓ Flashlight
- ⚓ Bookshelf or mantelpiece
- ⚓ Several pairs of shoes

Place the unlit flashlight on top of the bookshelf or the mantel. In front of it, make a pile of shoes. Make the room as dark as possible, then slowly walk toward the bookshelf or mantel. Can you see it? Do you stumble over the shoes? The shoes are like the rocks below a cliff.

Now turn on your flashlight "lighthouse," walk back across the room, and turn toward the bookshelf or mantel again. The bookshelf "cliff" is easier to see, of course, as are the shoe "rocks" below.

Offshore Dangers

Unpredictable shorelines were not the only cause of shipwrecks. Other dangers lurked just offshore. Without the aid of modern navigational equipment like *sonar* (a device that uses sound waves to detect obstacles), what lay beneath the water, such as unexpected shallow areas or submerged rocks, was a mystery to mariners. Ships could also be tossed about in rough waters or caught in unpredictable currents. Mariners relied on lighthouses to alert them to these dangerous areas. And when navigating through a thick fog, mariners used the reassuring sight of the lighthouse (and the sound of its booming foghorn!) to help them get their bearings.

Ouch! That Hurt!

One of the most dangerous underwater threats is a rocky *reef* — a hidden pile of jagged rocks in a shallow offshore area. Rocks are harder than the boards of a ship — and they don't move. Crashing into them could punch big holes in boats, causing them to flood and sink.

Make a rocky reef

What you need

⚓ Some small rocks

⚓ Aluminum pie pan or tray

⚓ Water

⚓ Red, blue, and green food coloring

⚓ Small plastic toy boat or piece of aluminum foil molded into a boat shape

Arrange the rocks in the bottom of the pie pan or tray, piling them up at irregular intervals. Make sure they're at least 1 inch (2.5 cm) below the rim. Fill the pan with water so you've covered the rocky mounds. Add a mix of the food coloring so the water turns a dark, dingy color. Try to navigate the boat through the water without hitting or nudging the rocky mounds. What happens? Because the water is so dark, the mounds are hard to avoid.

Now imagine you're the captain of a ship, navigating at night. How would you spot the rocks under the water? What might happen if the *prow* (front) of your boat ran into those jagged rocks?

The Treacherous Minots Ledge

Minots Ledge is a rocky reef just south of Boston. Dozens of ships have wrecked here, sending countless people to a watery grave. One of the worst shipwrecks happened in 1849, when the *Saint John*, loaded with Irish immigrants, approached the ledge. The ship struck the reef and quickly began to fall apart. There were only a few survivors. Ironically, people were trying to build a lighthouse on the rocky ledge (see pages 52 to 53), something that had never been done before. Unfortunately, it was not yet complete when the *Saint John* smashed into the reef.

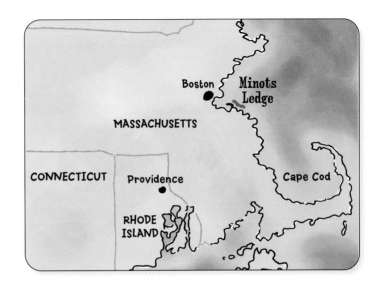

A Poet's Inspiration

The treacherous waters of Minots Ledge inspired one poet to write about it and its lighthouse. Below is an excerpt from that poem. What images do the words bring to mind? What does he compare the clouds to? How about the sound of the crashing waves?

Minots Ledge

Like spectral hounds across the sky
    The white clouds scud before the storm,
And naked in the howling night
    The red-eyed light-house lifts its form.
The waves with slippery fingers clutch
    The massive tower, and climb and fall,
And, muttering, growl with baffled rage
    Their curses on the sturdy wall.

—Fitz James O'Brien

Help! We're Stuck!

Another challenge to navigators was *sandbars* (or *bars*), long stretches of sand that pile up offshore. These bars can be partially exposed or completely covered at different times of the day, depending on the tides. What's more, they shift with the movement of the current (see page 14) and the waves, so they're not always where you expect them to be. If the submerged part of a ship were to hit a sandbar, the heavy ship could get stuck.

Before boats powered by steam engines began to appear, ships relied on the power of the wind to push against sails or the power of people to row. So if you got stuck on a sandbar, you couldn't simply put the boat's engine in reverse — the boat didn't have one! When a large two-masted sailing ship ran aground, there wasn't much those on board could do. If they were lucky, the ship would float again when the tide came in. Sometimes, however, these ships actually wrecked on the bar, and those on board didn't survive.

Lighthouse Legends & Lore

In addition to its beacon, the Boston Light (see page 7) also has an enormous bell, rung to warn ships on foggy days. Despite its immense size, however, the bell cannot be heard in one area just a few miles (km) east of the lighthouse, which mariners call the "ghost walk." Not even a team of students from Massachusetts Institute of Technology, who studied this phenomenon for a summer, could solve the mystery!

Cape Disappointment Lighthouse, Washington

How does that name sound for a lighthouse? One can only imagine the "disappointment" the residents of this area were referring to — shipwrecks and loss of life. This lighthouse is perched at the southern end of Washington State, in the town of Ilwaco. It is here that the Columbia River meets the Pacific Ocean. Large underwater sandbars build up here due to the movement of the water. Ships would often run aground, and passengers would find themselves jumping overboard to save their lives. In fact, the *Oriole*, the ship carrying supplies to build the lighthouse, wrecked before it could reach land. The lighthouse was finally built in 1856, and it is still active today.

Rocky Top, Home Beam...

Cyclops!

🏃 TRY IT! 🏃 Name a lighthouse!

The names of many lighthouses reflect the dangerous histories of their locations: Cape Disappointment, Graves Ledge, Shipwreck Point, Ram Island Ledge, and Old Cape Spear. With a group of friends, pick one of these locations (or make up your own location's name). Have each person write a brief description of an event that you think could have taken place there to give the location its name (make it as vivid as you can!). Then create a name for the lighthouse that would guard its shores. Vote on which story you think sounds the most realistic and which name you like best. Try it again with another location!

Rough Waters Ahead!

Rough seas are yet another maritime danger. Sometimes the sea is rough because of a storm. Lighthouses can help alert navigators about areas that are dangerous during bad weather. A rocky reef, clearly visible when the seas are calm, might be hidden under the crashing waves of a big storm, for example.

Lighthouses can also help warn mariners of water that is predictably, well, unpredictable! The direction in which water moves is called the *current*. If one current is moving one way, and another current is moving in a different direction, the area where the two currents meet is very rough and ships get tossed around. A lighthouse marking this area of rough seas can alert navigators as to what is ahead.

Create a rough current

What you need

⚓ Your toy or foil boat (see page 10)
⚓ Sink full of water

You can easily re-create and observe rough water for yourself. Place the boat in the water, then gently move your hand in the water in one direction to create a current. The boat should bob smoothly along. Now with your other hand, move the water in the opposite direction, while still moving the first hand. How does your boat move now?

Sound the Foghorn!

As you saw from the wreck of the *Anglo-Saxon* (see page 8), a thick fog can be very dangerous. Fog typically develops when warm air and cool air collide. The warm air condenses to form tiny water droplets, and a fog then develops over that area, blinding the navigator from seeing the land and any other dangers that lie ahead.

Unfortunately, lights don't always help in the fog. That's because the beam of light reflects off those little droplets, bouncing back to your eyes and actually making it harder to see. The next time you're in a car on a night when it's foggy or raining heavily, ask the driver to show you the difference between driving with the regular headlights or with the high beams. Which makes it easier to see? Chances are, it's the regular lights!

When light doesn't help, the navigator's next best hope is to hear a loud, blaring sound. Most lighthouses, therefore, are also equipped with loud horns, aptly called *foghorns*. The horn helps mariners pinpoint direction, as well as gauge distances.

TRY IT! See how sound travels

Can you think of a way to demonstrate to a friend how a foghorn can sometimes be more helpful than a beam of light, using a flashlight and a door you can close between the two of you? Remember, light waves can pass through some things, but not all; sound waves can pass through many things, even solid objects.

Answer: You can't shine the beam of light through the closed door, but you can call to your friend through it!

A MATTER OF LIGHT — OR DEATH!

Sandy Hook Light, New Jersey — America's Oldest Original Lighthouse!

The Sandy Hook Light sits on a spit of land that juts off the north New Jersey coast into New York Harbor. It was built in 1764, and although not very tall (85 feet/26 m), it has proved to be extremely sturdy. Instead of a circular shape, the building has an octagonal shape. Just as they did with the Boston Light (see page 7), colonial fighters actually tried to destroy the lighthouse during the American Revolution, but the original lighthouse still stands in operation today!

For many years, the lighthouse was actually called the New York Lighthouse because New York merchants had raised the money to build it. New York and New Jersey wrestled with the ownership of the lighthouse. In 1789, the newly formed United States government solved their dispute by taking control of the lighthouse. Today, the lighthouse is part of the Gateway National Recreation Area, and it is operated by the U.S. Coast Guard (see page 86).

✕TRY IT!✕ Write a captain's log entry

In his ship's log, the fictitious Captain Smythe described a dangerous storm at sea and expressed the relief he and his crew felt at the sight of the "beacon of light from the shore." Ship captains often kept a journal like this of their experiences during long voyages at sea.

How might a captain feel surrounded by a thick, blinding fog with no land in sight? What might he say about the reassuring sight of a lighthouse's beam sweeping across the water to reveal rough waters or a solid rock cliff straight ahead? Imagine what one of these experiences would be like and write a log entry from the ship captain's point of view.

CHAPTER 2

Light It Up!

* The Science Behind Those Big Lights *

It might not seem like a big deal to place a giant lightbulb at the top of a huge tower, creating a powerful beam of light. But think again. A lighthouse lamp has to provide steady light for many hours. It has to reach way out across the ocean and be seen for miles (km). And it has to be a clear signal, easily distinguished in all kinds of weather.

Long before electricity was invented, people had only one source of light — fire. And in fact, historians believe that the very first lighthouses were probably no more than bonfires burning high on a cliff. As people's knowledge of science and their understanding of the principles of light developed, a lighthouse lamp evolved from an open flame into a complicated lens with reflecting prisms and, eventually, to an automated electric light. Let's explore what has made lighthouses shine so brightly over the hundreds of years they've been in use.

More Wood — Now!

Early bonfire lighthouses were not easy to keep up because someone had to continuously add wood to them. Not only was this a tiring task, but it also used a lot of fuel! Imagine having a roaring fire every night, from sundown to sunup. Think of all the trees you'd need to chop down to keep the fire lit. There had to be a better way!

The first advance in the design of lighthouses was to use candlelight. A candle burns slowly as the flame makes its way down the wick. It doesn't have to be watched constantly, but instead can be checked every few hours to make sure it hasn't gone out. But how could that tiny light atop a tower possibly help a ship out on the ocean? Check out the spider lamp to see!

The Spider Lamp

One way to increase the strength of the light was to light more than one candle, or wick. One lamp of this type was called a *spider lamp* — count the number of wicks (and think about how many legs a spider has), and you can probably guess why! These lamps began to be used in lighthouses in the United States around 1790. Lighthouse keepers didn't much like them, though. The "lamp" was really just a pan of oil (for fuel) with the wicks stuck into it, and the burning fuel gave off a really strong and unpleasant smell. The fumes were so bad that a lighthouse keeper often had to leave the lighthouse in order to breathe!

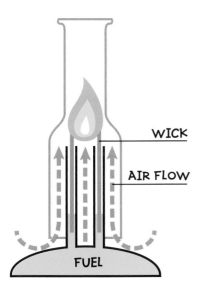

WICK

AIR FLOW

FUEL

No More Spiders!

Nobody liked the spider lamp — it was smelly, smoky, and not very efficient. In the early 1780s, a European inventor named François-Pierre Ami Argand (AR-gawn) came up with a solution. He created a hollow wick that sat in a fuel pan. That hollow wick did the trick! Why? Oxygen flowed around the wick, which created a sturdier, brighter flame that burned more cleanly. Argand's invention eventually made its way to the United States, and the Argand lamp was soon adopted in many lighthouses.

✶TRY IT!✶ See how light travels

To improve upon the very basic design of the spider lamp and develop a brighter (and less smelly!) lighthouse light, people had to first understand more about light and how it travels.

Grab a flashlight, and check out the same basic principles of light that people were beginning to understand at this time.

✷ Light comes from a specific source, and the light is brightest at that source. OK, so that's pretty easy to see from your flashlight's bulb.

✷ Light travels in straight lines, called *rays*. They move out from the source in all directions but always following a straight path. What is the shape of your flashlight's beam?

✷ As the light rays move away from the source, they begin to *diffuse*, or scatter, losing their intensity. Eventually, the light rays from your flashlight will spread so far out that you can't see them at all. That is why a beam of light will only stretch so far and no more — the light rays have diffused. You can probably see this effect a little bit along the edges of the flashlight's beam, for they will seem a bit fuzzier than the middle area of light.

Developing Light Reflectors

As you saw with fog (see page 15), light can reflect off objects and bounce back to your eyes, actually making it harder to see. But light reflection can be handy, too, because it can send more light out from the source, resulting in a brighter light. Once Argand invented his lamp, people began experimenting with reflectors. A reflector was easier to use with Argand's lamp than with a spider lamp because Argand's lamp had only one flame.

Historians aren't sure who came up with the reflector idea initially. But in the United States, the credit went to a retired sea captain named Winslow Lewis. He took Argand's lamp and put a curved mirror, or reflector, behind it. He showed his lamp to lighthouse officials, and soon after that, the Lewis lamp was in most lighthouses in the United States.

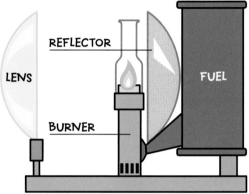

See the power of reflected light

What you need

⚓ Mirror

⚓ Darkened room

⚓ Towel or other large piece of fabric

⚓ Lamp with lampshade removed

Place the mirror in the room, then cover it with the towel or fabric. (If you choose a bathroom with a mirrored medicine cabinet, just open the door so that it won't yet reflect light.) Turn on the lamp. Look at a spot on the wall opposite the mirror and notice how bright it is.

Now unveil your mirror, and look at the spot again. What has happened to the beam of light?

A Poet's Inspiration

Henry Wadsworth Longfellow was a well-known American poet who lived in the 1800s. Here are a few verses from his poem "The Lighthouse." How many different ways does Longfellow talk about light in the poem?

The Lighthouse

The rocky ledge runs far into the sea,
　　And on its outer point, some miles away,
The lighthouse lifts its massive masonry,
　　A pillar of fire by night, of cloud by day.

And as the evening darkens, lo! how bright,
　　Through the deep purple of the twilight air,
Beams forth the sudden radiance of its light,
　　With strange, unearthly splendor in the glare!

No one alone: from each projecting cape
　　And perilous reef along the ocean's verge,
Starts into life a dim, gigantic shape,
　　Holding its lantern o'er the restless surge.

Steadfast, serene, immovable, the same,
　　Year after year, through all the silent night
Burns on forevermore that quenchless flame,
　　Shines on that inextinguishable night!

—Henry Wadsworth Longfellow

☀TRY IT!☀ Write a lighthouse poem

Start with a list of words that rhyme with *light*. Now how about words that rhyme with *shine* or *flame*? Think of other words to tell about a lighthouse. How about words that rhyme with *shore*, *waves*, or *tide*? Use your list of rhyming words to write your poem.

　　Create your poem in the shape of a lighthouse! Draw the outline, then write the first line at the top (it might only be one word). Add the next line (it might be two or three words). Continue composing your poem, creating longer lines at the base to complete the lighthouse's shape.

Lighthouse, Oh Lighthouse!

Lighthouse,
oh lighthouse,
Watching over the waves.
Lives of the sailors,
Oh, how you so save.
Shining and gleaming,
In the night sky.
Bright as a star,
With your watchful eye.
Guiding the ships,
All across the waves—
Lighthouse, oh lighthouse,
Your strength we so crave.
You get too little credit,
and never complain.
I am your keeper,
so let me explain.
When you turn on your beacon,
To watch over the sea,
What you must know is that
You're part of me.

You protect us all just like a big fire truck.
Your friends are the sea and the waves and the ducks.
You watch for us all and the ships and the shore—
And as your keeper, I could not ask for more.

— Nicolette Basiliere, age 14, and Andrea Racine, age 14

Portland Head Light, Maine

When you see a painting of a lighthouse, it just might be the Portland Head Light on Cape Elizabeth, Maine. Guiding ships into Portland Harbor since 1791, Portland Head Light is one of the most often-painted lighthouses in the United States! In fact, many people think it is the lighthouse that inspired Henry Wadsworth Longfellow to write the poem on page 21.

The lighthouse sits on the craggy coast outside the city of Portland. The tall, white tower is flanked on either side by red-roofed houses, which at one time were the home to the lighthouse keeper and his family. Over the years, the various keepers of this lighthouse have used many warning devices as foghorns, including trumpets, heavy bells, and even a cannon!

TRY IT! Create a lighthouse painting!

Discover why lighthouses are such a popular subject for paintings by creating your own original work of art. Work from a photo, if you like, or just let your imagination inspire you. Depending on where you live, you might even be able to use a real lighthouse as your subject! Think about the mood you would like your painting to evoke — do you want a dramatic scene with dark storm clouds and crashing waves or a peaceful one with blue skies and a tranquil sea? For bold images, use bright-colored tempera paints; try watercolors for subtler effects.

A Bigger, Brighter Light

In 1822, a French physicist named Augustin-Jean Fresnel (FREY-nel) delivered the next development in lighthouse light technology. And it was a huge one, producing a beam five times more powerful than the reflector lamp!

Light Will Bend!

Fresnel had a fascination with light, and for years he had performed complex experiments to prove his theories on bending and reflecting light beams.

Fresnel felt that there had to be a way to stop a beam of light from diffusing (see page 19), thereby making it brighter. He experimented with using lenses of different shapes and thicknesses to actually bend, or *refract*, the rays of light from the lighthouse lamp. This technique concentrated the rays horizontally, making them brighter so they could be seen from farther away.

"If you cannot saw with a file or file with a saw, you will be no good as an experimenter."
—Augustin-Jean Fresnel, inventor of the Fresnel lens

Bend a beam of light

What you need
- Flashlight
- Table
- Lens (pair of eyeglasses or a magnifying glass)
- Dark room

Place the flashlight against the edge of the table as shown so that the beam is concentrated on the table's surface. Then hold the lens in front of the flashlight, about 3" to 4" (7.5 to 10 cm) away. Begin to move the lens back and forth. You'll see that the light shining *through* the lens moves, but the light shining *from* the flashlight does not. This movement is the light rays bending as they pass through the lens!

The Fresnel Lens

Fresnel's experiments resulted in the design of a complex lens, which replaced the reflectors on the Lewis lamps. The Fresnel lens looks like a huge glass beehive! It's oval in shape, with "honeycombs" of glass prisms surrounding a single lamp at the center. The prisms concentrate the beam of light so the beam is much brighter than at its source.

Fresnel lenses come in six *orders*, or variations of brightness. A first-order lens is the brightest and biggest; a second-order lens is the next brightest, and so on. The Fresnel lens greatly extended the visibility of lighthouse lights; depending on the size of the lens, these lights could be seen for 20 miles (6 k) or more.

Eventually, the Fresnel lens became *the* lens in lighthouses, first in Europe, and then in North America, and it remained so in the United States until the 1940s. Many lighthouses still have their original Fresnel lens intact (although most are no longer used); others have been removed and placed in museums.

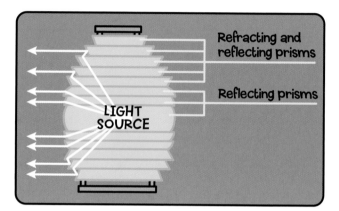

LIGHT SOURCE

Refracting and reflecting prisms

Reflecting prisms

Concentrate a beam of light

What you need

⚓ Page magnifier (available from office-supply stores)   ⚓ Darkened room   ⚓ Flashlight

You can use a simple page magnifier to see the effect of a Fresnel lens. This plastic sheet is covered on one side with slightly raised circles, one circle inside another. These circles create multiple lenses that work a bit like the prisms of a Fresnel lens.

In the darkened room, shine the flashlight at a wall. Notice the size of the circle of light on the wall. What happens when you place the page magnifier in front of the flashlight beam? The lenses bend the rays of light so they don't diffuse (see page 19), but instead are concentrated into a bigger, brighter beam. Just imagine the effect of a huge Fresnel lens magnifying the beam of light from the top of a lighthouse!

Shine a Light On ...

NAVESINK LIGHT STATION, NEW JERSEY — America's First Fresnel Lens!

The Navesink Light Station, site of the Navesink Twin Lights, reflects the history of America's lighthouses. First built in 1828, the two towers stood about 320 feet (98 m) apart. Unfortunately, they were not well constructed, and so rather quickly began to fall apart. Before they did so, however, they were actually fitted with Fresnel lenses — a major accomplishment for this time. The towers were rebuilt in 1862 with much sturdier stones. One tower was square, and one tower was octagonal, and the towers were connected. With a first-order Fresnel lens in one tower and a second-order lens in the other, the Navesink Twin Lights were the brightest lights in the United States. The lighthouse was deactivated in 1952, and today it is a museum.

Learn the Lingo!

light station: this term refers to all the buildings on the site (the lighthouse, the keeper's house, etc.) as well as to the property itself.

TRY IT! Create lights of different brightnesses

Compare your own lights of different brightnesses. Start with one flashlight or desk lamp. Place another one beside it. Then another, then another. How much brighter can you go? For fun, place one, then two, then three lamps in a window. See how far away a friend or someone in your family can view the lamps outside at night!

Makapuu Point Light, Hawaii — The Biggest Fresnel Lens Ever!

The biggest Fresnel lens ever put in an American lighthouse was in Hawaii at Makapuu Point on the island of Oahu. Installed in 1909, the original Fresnel lens is still in operation today. The lens is about 16 feet (5 m) high and about 8½ feet (2.5 m) around! The Fresnel lens at Makapuu Point is so powerful that it is visible for 28 miles (47 km)!

With an adult's help, figure out a point on a map that is that distance away from your house. If this lighthouse were there, its beam of light would be visible from your yard!

Lighthouses in Hawaii?

Yes, even on the islands of Hawaii! In the late 1700s, world travel had gone beyond simply sailing from the shores of Europe to the east coast of North America. Ships were also traveling between America's west coast and Asia, as well as to the islands in the Pacific. Whaling had become big business, and many American ships used the Hawaiian Islands as their base. The people of Hawaii were beginning to ship goods, too, like sugar and pineapple.

Check out a world map, and you'll see that Hawaii, located right in the middle of the northern Pacific Ocean, is an ideal stop for ships traveling between the Americas and Asia. With so many ships coming and going, a lighthouse in the middle of the Pacific Ocean made a lot of sense.

In 1905, the United States Lighthouse Board (see page 86) warned in a report that "… there is not a single light on the whole northern coast of the Hawaiian Islands to guide ships or warn them of the approach to land, after a voyage of several thousand miles (km)." The Makapuu Point Light made traveling across the Pacific much safer — and surer!

Blinking Lights

Which type of light do you think would get your attention at a traffic intersection — a flashing light or a steady one? Ask an adult who drives and see what he or she says. Chances are, they'll say the blinking light, because the movement catches their eye. Well, this same idea works when you're on a ship too. So not all lighthouse lights are a fixed (steady) beam.

This chart describes some different ways that lighthouse lights can vary or change their intensity. These different lights also help mariners to distinguish one lighthouse from another. Sometimes several lighthouses are closely spaced along the same coast; different flashes help mariners determine their location and navigate accordingly.

Learn the Lingo!

To **occult** something means to not expose it or, to shut it off from view.

To **eclipse** something means to darken or partially obscure it.

Type of Light	What It Does
Fixed	one, steady beam of light
Flashing	a single flash at regular intervals
Group Flashing	two or more flashes, at regular intervals
Occulting	a steady beam of light, with regular intervals of an eclipse, or a partial beam of light
Group Occulting	a steady beam of light, with regular intervals of more than one eclipse or partial light
Fixed and Flashing	a steady beam of light, then at regular intervals, a brighter flash of light
Fixed and Group Flashing	a steady beam of light, then at regular intervals, a series of two or more brighter flashes of light

See what I mean?

wink wink

Create different lighthouse lights

What you need

⚓ Flashlight or two   ⚓ Sheet of paper   ⚓ A friend

How many of the different beams and flashes of light listed on page 27 can you make? Spin your flashlight (or turn it on and off) to create the flashes and partially obscure the beam with a sheet of paper (or your hand) to make the eclipses. Can your friend tell which flash you're re-creating? Now it's your turn to guess!

Lighthouse Legends & Lore

Lighthouses are frequently said to be haunted, and one of the best known lighthouse ghosts inhabits Michigan's now-abandoned Waugoshance Light on Lake Michigan. Lighthouse keeper John Herman was first stationed at Waugoshance in 1885. Herman was well known for his practical jokes and one August evening, so the story goes, he locked his assistant in the lamp room and headed out for a walk. Before the assistant could free himself from the room, he watched Herman stroll along the pier — and then suddenly disappear, never to be seen again!

After Herman's disappearance, strange occurrences began in the lighthouse. Chairs would be kicked out mysteriously from under people. Doors would suddenly open or lock by themselves. From time to time, the new keeper would find that "someone" had shoveled the boiler full of coal. The Waugoshance Light was abandoned when it was replaced by the White Shoal Light, but many people say it was really abandoned because no keeper was willing to share the lighthouse with the ghost of John Herman.

It's Electric!

In 1879, Thomas Edison introduced people in the United States to what would become his landmark invention: the electric lightbulb. No longer was a fuel, like oil, needed to keep a lantern lit. And no longer did people need to light matches to light their lamps. Instead, a lightbulb and electricity did all the work for them.

An electric light was so much brighter than a candle flame that the way people looked at light would never be the same again — nor would lighthouses remain the same. When paired with a Fresnel lens, the light shining from a lighthouse now had the power of about *4.5 billion candles*! Slowly, the lamps inside Fresnel lenses were replaced by electric lights. By the 1930s, all lighthouses in North America had been electrified.

Shine a Light On ...

STATUE OF LIBERTY, NEW YORK — The First Electric U.S. Lighthouse!

The first lighthouse in the United States to be electrified was the Statue of Liberty. That's right — for the first few years of her existence, Lady Liberty was a working lighthouse! Her torch, held hundreds of feet (m) above the water, contained nine electric lamps that could be seen 24 miles (38 km) out to sea, and from 1886 to 1902, it guided ships into New York Harbor. No longer an active lighthouse, the Statue of Liberty remains a much-visited tourist attraction maintained by the National Park Service.

More Lighthouse Improvements:
Automation and Beacons

As lighthouse lamps were becoming electrified, they were also becoming automated, meaning they would go on automatically. No longer was someone needed to light the lamp.

And as new technologies in electric lights were developed, many Fresnel lenses were replaced by aeromarine beacons. These bright lights were originally created to light up airports. In the mid-1940s, after World War II, they were being installed in lighthouses! Two aeromarine beacons would be placed back to back, then the joined lights would turn, or rotate. From a distance, the rotating lights looked as if they were flashing. Many lighthouses, however, still have their Fresnel lenses.

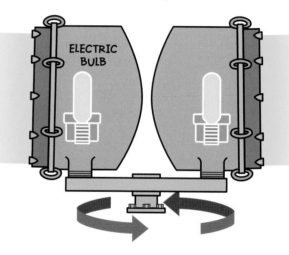

ELECTRIC BULB

Make a blinking beacon

What you need
⚓ Stiff paper
⚓ Tape
⚓ Flashlight
⚓ Darkened room
⚓ A friend

Place a piece of stiff paper three-quarters of the way around the rim of the flashlight as shown and tape it in place. Hold the flashlight up or down (not out in front of you). In a darkened room, rotate the flashlight and notice how the beam changes. Now have your friend turn the flashlight as you stand a distance from it. How does the light change? Does it appear to "blink" or "flash"?

Tower Power!

✳ Exploring Tower Lighthouses ✳

When you think of a lighthouse, you probably picture a tall tower, standing watch over a beach, with a light at the top. When you see paintings of lighthouses, they probably show one of these tower lights. Tower lighthouses are the most common types (to discover some others, see pages 57 to 70). Often located in a lovely scenic spot, there is something romantic about these tall structures, probably one of the reasons people enjoy painting them. And there is something compelling about them, rising more than 100 feet (30 m) above the sea, casting long shadows on the beach, often with an air of mystery about them. These tall stone monuments link us to our nautical past, when tall ships traveled the oceans to every corner of the globe. Although they look like simple structures, there is much more to these towers than first meets the eye. Let's explore them!

Standing Tall!

The first thing you notice about a tower lighthouse is, of course, its height! A tower lighthouse is usually the tallest structure for miles (km) around. Imagine a building with 16 floors, and you have the height of a typical tower lighthouse. Or imagine you and your friends standing on each other's shoulders. You'd need 40 friends to reach the top!

End-to-end lighthouse

What you need

⚓ 20 sheets of paper, 8½" x 11" (22 cm x 28 cm)

⚓ Tape

⚓ Colored pencils

To get the idea of the height of a lighthouse, make a paper one on the ground. Lay the sheets of paper out on the floor, taping them end to end as you go. Do you think that's long? Well, you'd need to add another 140 sheets to equal the height of a 160-foot (49-m) lighthouse! For now, though, draw a lighthouse on the paper you have. With adult help, tape the lighthouse drawing to your wall, from floor to ceiling.

The Better to See You!

Why were tower lights built so tall? Why, the better to see their bright lights from far out at sea, of course! The rays of light from a shorter lighthouse would not shine as far out over the water. The beam from a taller lighthouse reaches much farther, and therefore alerts sailors much sooner when they are approaching the coast or a hazardous area, giving them more time to react and change course.

See light diffuse into water

What you need
⚓ Flashlight
⚓ Bathroom

You can see the effect of building a tall tower with this simple experiment. Take the flashlight into the bathroom. Fill the sink with water, then turn off the lights and make the room as dark as possible. Holding the flashlight just above the level of the water, shine it toward the back of the sink. Where does some of the light fall? Remember that rays of light diffuse, or spread out vertically and horizontally (see page 19). You can see that some of the light rays have "diffused" into the water.

Now keep shining the flashlight in the same direction but hold it up higher. When a beam of light is higher, more of the light shines directly out to sea, so sailors can see it from farther away.

The View's Great from Up Here!

When you want to get a better look at something off in the distance, what's the first thing you do? Stand on your tiptoes to make yourself taller, of course! Or how about when you hike up a steep trail or ride the elevator to the top of a skyscraper? You are rewarded with an amazing view at the top! The higher up you go, the farther you can see.

So another reason a tower lighthouse is so tall is for the excellent view the keeper has from the very top. For a lighthouse keeper standing on the shore, the distance to the horizon is about 3 miles (5 km). The higher he or she goes above sea level, however, the farther he or she can see. On a clear day, that same keeper at the top of a 150-foot (45-m) lighthouse can look out across the ocean for close to 16 miles (26 km). From that height, it's much easier to spot ships or mariners in distress or to see oncoming storms!

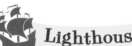

Lighthouse Legends & Lore

Tillamook Rock Light in Oregon was built in the late 1800s on a towering rock that juts out into the Pacific Ocean. Early settlers noticed that the Native Americans in this area tended to stay away from this rock, for they believed that it possessed evil spirits. See if you think it sounds cursed!

Building the lighthouse was not an easy task. The rock's height and jagged, slippery surface made it difficult to work on. The surf constantly beat upon the rock, sending up sprays of water and rocky debris. In fact, one of the men originally assigned to survey the rock slipped and fell into the water. His assistant dove in after him, but the surveyor was never found.

Lighthouse keepers never enjoyed working there, and the lighthouse was nicknamed Terrible Tilly. Along with the foul weather and treacherous landscape, lighthouse keepers often described ghostly moans and groans coming up the stairwell!

Michigan Island Light, Wisconsin

The Apostle Islands National Park off the coast of northern Wisconsin in Lake Superior is a popular vacation destination. Visitors can see several lighthouses, including the oldest one in this area — Michigan Island Light. Built in 1880, the cast-iron tower is not the original lighthouse built here. The tower that stands here today originally came from a spot in Pennsylvania along the Delaware River. The first lighthouse was a stone tower with an attached home, built in 1857. The cast-iron tower is taller than the original stone tower, and today it still shines its light over the lake.

A Hike Out to Sea!

From the Pilot Island Light, off the eastern coast of Wisconsin, comes this stirring tale of rescue by the lighthouse keeper. This lighthouse guards the Port des Morts (Death's Door) Passage on Lake Michigan. On a stormy night in 1892, keeper Martin Knudsen saw the wreck of the sailing ship *A.P. Nichols* offshore. In the dark of night, he started out to the ship on foot, making his way over several *shoals* (see page 60), or sandy ridges. Despite rough seas — including waves up to his neck in places! — he reached the ship and guided all of the passengers back to the shore.

Stairs, Stairs ... and More Stairs!

Lantern room

Watch room

So, how do you get to the top of a tower light? You have to walk! And depending on how tall the tower is, it's not always an easy chore.

When many of America's lighthouses were built, electricity had yet to be invented. There were no such things as elevators. So lighthouses were equipped with staircases — long, spiraling staircases. This diagram shows the spiral staircase inside Bodie Island Light in North Carolina, near Nags Head. You have to climb 214 steps to get to the top!

Entry door

TRY IT! Climb a lighthouse

Or at least the equivalent of one! Count the steps in a flight of stairs at your house, apartment building, or school. Figure out how many times you'd have to walk those stairs to get to the top of a lighthouse with 214 steps. Then try walking those 214 steps (you'll have to walk up and down to make the total). How do your legs feel?

Let's see... 214 stairs, divide by 4, that's 53.5 times.

Spiral staircases are not only tiring because they go up — but because they also go in circles. If you *really* want to know how it would feel to climb that spiral staircase, you'll have to go around and around something as you take your steps. Walk around the trunk of a tree or a table as you count the 214 steps. How do you feel? If you feel dizzy, you're not alone! Walking around and around a spiral staircase is not easy. Now imagine a lighthouse keeper walking up and down all these stairs at least once a day to make sure the light was lit!

Still Lighting the Way!

Bodie Island Light, North Carolina

Today, the Outer Banks of North Carolina is a beach vacationer's paradise. But hundreds of years ago, the rocky shoals and shallow waters of Oregon Inlet there wrecked so many ships, the area became known as the "Graveyard of the Atlantic." So the U.S. government decided that a lighthouse had to be built. The first one was not very tall (only 54 feet/17 m) or sturdy, so a taller one was built not long after. Then the Civil War erupted, and that lighthouse was blown up. Finally, in 1872, the lighthouse that stands on Bodie Island today was built. The 156-foot-tall (48-m) tower is still warning ships of the offshore hazards along this section of the North Carolina coast.

The Top Five!

The diagram below shows the height of North America's five tallest lighthouses. How does the tallest lighthouse on the list compare to the paper lighthouse you made on page 32?

Find these lighthouses on the map on pages 90 to 91. Think about what their heights tell you about the land in these locations and then turn the page to see if you are right!

| Cape Lookout Light Cape Lookout, NC 169 feet (52 m) | Absecon Light Atlantic City, NJ 171 feet (52.5 m) | Barnegat Light Long Beach Island, NJ 172 feet (53 m) | Ponce de Leon Inlet Light Ponce Inlet, FL 175 feet (54 m) | Cape Hatteras Light Cape Hatteras, NC 193 feet (59 m) |

A Short Lighthouse Can be Tall!

A lighthouse doesn't need to be tall to be effective — if it is sitting on a cliff! The tall lighthouses listed on page 37 are on low ground. They need to be built tall because no high peaks of land are nearby. Remember the Makapuu Point Light in Hawaii (see page 26)? It's only 46 feet (14 m). Yet it is 420 feet (129 m) *above sea level* because it sits on top of a tall cliff.

Still Lighting the Way!

Point Vicente Light, California

Although not as tall as its East Coast cousins, Point Vicente Light near Los Angeles is just as evocative. Perched on a cliff more than 100 feet (31 m) above the Pacific Ocean, the lighthouse is surrounded by palm trees and rugged coastline. This lighthouse has even been featured in the movies! (Not too surprising, with Hollywood right nearby.) Since 1926, its powerful light has swept out over the Catalina Channel, warning mariners about the treacherous rocky shoals just offshore.

![TRY IT!] Describe the view!

Imagine you're standing at the top of a lighthouse tower, admiring the breathtaking view! You can see out to sea for miles and miles (km), and down either end of the beach as well. You can even see the scenery on the other side of the lighthouse, which could be houses or trees or maybe an inland bay.

   Describe what the sights look like from the top of a tower light. Here's a fun way to start! Write down your ideas by using the letters of the word *lighthouse*. Draw the outline of a lighthouse tower, write each letter inside, then write your description outside the lighthouse.

Lighthouse Legends & Lore

The Point Vicente Light is also said to be haunted! People living near the lighthouse didn't like the lighthouse's bright light, so the windows were painted white. Today, some people claim to see the silhouette of a woman walking behind the painted glass. They believe she might be the wife of the lighthouse's first keeper, who slipped off the cliff on a foggy night.

Color-Coded Lighthouses

Turn to the map on pages 90 to 91 and find these three lighthouses: Cape Hatteras Light, Cape Lookout Light, and Bodie Island Light. What do you notice? They are *very* close together along the North Carolina shore. Now imagine you are a sailor, approaching that section of the coast. If all three lighthouses were white, how would you know which lighthouse you were looking at?

When you look at these three lighthouses side by side, however, you'll see there's an easy solution to this problem! Many tower lighthouses have their own distinguishing patterns so that, in the daylight at least, sailors can tell them apart. It's like a code to mariners out at sea.

Not all lighthouses have a black-and-white pattern. Some lighthouse patterns are in red. What color would *you* choose to stand out against the blue of the sea and sky, the pale sand, and the green of the trees? How about against the dark colors of a rocky cliff?

THINK ABOUT IT!

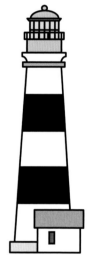

If you see a swirl of black and white, you're near Cape Hatteras.

If you see diamonds, you're at Cape Lookout.

Thick vertical bands of black and white identify the Bodie Island Light.

How might navigators tell these lighthouses apart at night? See page 27 for a hint, then check the bottom of the page to see if you're right!

If you guessed that these lighthouses have different flashing lights so they can be identified easily, you're right. See RESOURCES on page 92 to visit their web sites and find out what the different flashing light patterns are.

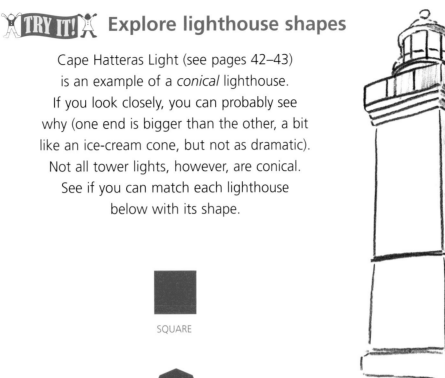

🙌 TRY IT! 🙌 Explore lighthouse shapes

Cape Hatteras Light (see pages 42–43)
is an example of a *conical* lighthouse.
If you look closely, you can probably see
why (one end is bigger than the other, a bit
like an ice-cream cone, but not as dramatic).
Not all tower lights, however, are conical.
See if you can match each lighthouse
below with its shape.

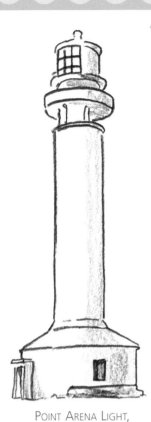

POINT ARENA LIGHT,
POINT ARENA, CALIFORNIA

SQUARE

OCTAGON

PYRAMID

CYLINDER

DUNKIRK LIGHT,
POINT GRATIOT, NEW YORK

BADDECK HARBOUR LIGHT,
CAPE BRETON ISLAND,
NOVA SCOTIA

GRAYS HARBOR LIGHT,
POINT CHEHALIS,
WASHINGTON

Point Arena Light, cylinder; Dunkirk Light, square; Baddeck
Harbour Light, pyramid; Grays Harbor Light, octagon

Make the Cape Hatteras Light

Create a model of the lighthouse at Cape Hatteras, complete with its dramatic black and white stripes!

What you need

- ⚓ Cardboard paper-towel tube
- ⚓ Old newspaper
- ⚓ Paintbrush
- ⚓ Tempera paints, black and white
- ⚓ Empty thread spool
- ⚓ Pencil
- ⚓ Thick paper, like card stock or an old manilla file folder
- ⚓ Scissors
- ⚓ Glue or tape
- ⚓ Aluminum pie plate filled with sand or soil
- ⚓ Small rocks or pebbles (optional)

What you do

1. First, look at the spirals on the paper-towel tube. Do they remind you of anything? (Look back at page 40). They resemble the spirals on the Cape Hatteras Light! Cover your work surface with newspaper. Paint the spirals in an alternating pattern of black and white. You might paint all the black spirals first, then all the white spirals. Wait for the paint to dry.

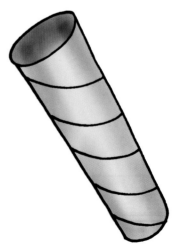

2. Paint the empty thread spool black, too, leaving a round space unpainted on one side (that's your light!). Let it dry as well.

3. Place the tube on the paper and draw a circle around it, about ¼" (5 mm) larger than the tube. Cut it out.

4. Center the paper-towel tube on the paper circle and tape or glue them together. Flip the model over so the circle is at the top. Glue the spool in the center of the circle.

5. Place your lighthouse model in the pan, molding the sand around the bottom to secure the tube. Add some small rocks or pebbles, if you like.

Lighthouse Legends & Lore

Theodosia Burr Alton was the daughter of Aaron Burr, who served as vice president under Thomas Jefferson from 1801 to 1805. In 1812, Theodosia was traveling by ship from her home in South Carolina to New York City to visit her father. Her ship, *The Patriot*, disappeared off the coast of Cape Hatteras. Did the ship get caught in a fierce storm? Or was it attacked by pirates? No one really knows! However, even today, many people claim to see Theodosia's ghost, walking among the dunes beneath the Cape Hatteras Light!

Ponce de Leon Inlet Light, Florida

Offering a sweeping view of the Florida coastline from
Daytona Beach to New Symrna Beach, the Ponce de Leon
Inlet Light is one tall tower! At 175 feet (54 m), not only
is it Florida's tallest lighthouse, it is also one of the top five
tallest in the U.S. (see page 37). And it's a sturdy one too —
when rocked by a major earthquake in 1886, it stood
strong. Although now privately owned, it is still used as a
navigational aid.

A Writer's Inspiration

Stephen Crane, author of the classic American novel *The Red Badge of Courage*, was
in a shipwreck off the Florida coast in 1896. During the night, Crane, the captain,
and two companions rowed ashore in a small dinghy, guided to safety by the Ponce
de Leon Inlet Light. Crane later wrote one of his most famous short stories, called
"The Open Boat," about this terrifying experience.

In this excerpt, the men catch their first glimpse of the lighthouse. Crane,
who had been onboard the ship as an undercover reporter investigating rumors of
smuggling, is the "correspondent" in the story. How does this beacon of safety
appear to the men when viewed from far out at sea?

The Open Boat

"See it?" said the captain. "No," said the correspondent, slowly, "I didn't see
anything." "Look again," said the captain. He pointed. "It's exactly in that direction."
At the top of another wave, the correspondent did as he was bid, and this time
his eyes chanced on a small still thing on the edge of the swaying horizon. It was
precisely like the point of a pin. It took an anxious eye to find a lighthouse so tiny.
. . . .
… Meanwhile the light-house had been growing slowly larger. It had now
almost assumed color, and appeared like a little gray shadow on the sky. The man
at the oars could not be prevented from turning his head rather often to try for a
glimpse of this little gray shadow.

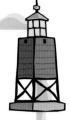

CHAPTER 4

Sturdy as She Goes!

✴ Building a Long-Lasting Tower Lighthouse ✴

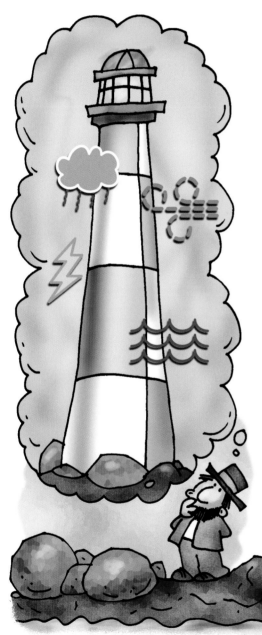

A tower lighthouse (see pages 31 to 44) might look like a simple structure, but building one was a complicated project! Engineers had to design a structure that could withstand steady winds and coastal storms like hurricanes and, in some cases, also hold up to the pounding of ocean waves day after day. The structure had to support a huge light at a height that mariners could easily spot from a great distance. And because lighthouses were built on shorelines, they were constructed on anything ranging from soft, sandy soil to a solid rock ledge. Often the lighthouse had to provide warm, dry accommodations for the keeper and his or her family. Each location had its own conditions, but the safety of both the keeper and the passing ships always had to be considered carefully.

Step into a lighthouse-builder's shoes to explore some of the technical considerations involved in building these sturdy structures that, in many cases, have stood strong for more than 100 years!

In Search of the Perfect Tower

Building a tower lighthouse could be "hit or miss": Sometimes the lighthouse was built to be sturdy enough to withstand the powerful wind and water; other times, the structure had to be modified because it wasn't adequate. Even worse, sometimes it needed to be replaced entirely because it had been destroyed in a storm. Lighthouse designers and builders were always looking for ways to make lighthouses more stable and sturdy.

Tower-Builder's Checklist

Although each lighthouse location was different, engineers, designers, and builders needed to consider certain principles of design before building any tower lighthouse.

You might recognize the name of author Robert Louis Stevenson, and perhaps you've read some of his classic adventure stories such as *Treasure Island* and *Kidnapped*. What you might not know is that Stevenson came from a family of famous lighthouse designers! His grandfather, uncle, and several cousins were all lighthouse engineers in Scotland.

Let's listen in as David Stevenson, who designed close to 30 lighthouses in his lifetime, explains to his young nephew Robert Louis how to make the perfect tower lighthouse.

1 First, Robert my boy, we must think about the tower's **center of gravity**, the place where the structure's weight is equally balanced in all directions. It should be as close to the ground as possible.

2 Next we consider the building's **mass** (its size and weight combined). It must be sufficient so that the tower can't be pushed over by high winds and pounding waves.

That makes sense!

3 The best shape for the tower is a tall cone. The upper portion should curve in slightly so the waves will be projected back on themselves. Lighthouses that are hit over and over by waves - we call these "wave-swept towers" - are best when constructed this way.

4 It helps if the outer surface of the tower is smooth so the water just quickly runs back down. There is less wind resistance, too.

Oooh!

5 And finally, young Robert, the tower should be tall enough to keep the lantern clear of water and salt spray. After all, we wouldn't want the flame to be kidnapped by the water, would we?

Kidnapped?

"It can be seen from these considerations that a wave-swept lighthouse is a marvel of ingenuity and that it needs to be, for the forces against which the lighthouse engineer pits his wits are well-nigh incredble."
—from *A History of Lighthouses* by Patrick Beaver

STURDY AS SHE GOES!

Find the center of gravity

What you need

⚓ Pencil

⚓ Your finger

⚓ Eraser or other small object

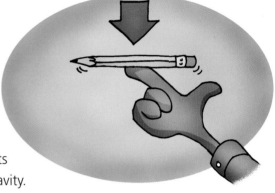

Every object has a *center of gravity*. This is the place on the object where its weight is distributed equally, allowing it to balance and stay upright.

    Balance the pencil on your finger as shown. The point where the pencil balances is its center of gravity. Now change that center of gravity. Place the eraser or other small object on one end of the pencil. Does the pencil balance at the same place? No! You have to readjust the pencil on your finger to make it balance again. You've changed the pencil's center of gravity.

    You can change your center of gravity, too! When you're skiing or skateboarding, for example, you typically bend your knees. This position lowers your center of gravity, giving you better balance while you're moving, so that you stay upright.

♨ TRY IT! ♨ Conical? Check!

Use David Stevenson's checklist on pages 46 to 47 to evaluate one of his own wave-swept tower lighthouses! Take a close look at this illustration of Dubh Artach Light in Scotland, built in 1872. (You won't be able to determine the building's center of gravity or its mass by sight, so just skip those two.) Do its shape, height, and surface pass the test?

Test a cone vs. a cylinder

What you need

- ⚓ Old party hat (optional)
- ⚓ Sheets of paper
- ⚓ Tape
- ⚓ Scissors
- ⚓ Pencil

You've probably noticed that most tower lighthouses are wider on the bottom than they are at the top. Compare cylinder and cone shapes to see why this conical design is more effective.

If you have an old party hat, it will work perfectly for the cone. If not, roll a sheet of paper into a cone shape and tape the edge, then trim the bottom so the cone sits flat. Trace the bottom onto another sheet of paper — that circle is the diameter of your cone. Roll another piece of paper into a cylinder of the same diameter and tape its edge. Now place both the cylinder and the cone on a table, side by side, and give them a blast of "ocean breeze"!

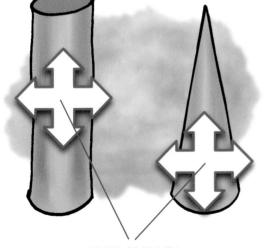

CENTER OF GRAVITY

Back to ... Center of Gravity!

The cylinder shape is the same size all the way around. Its *center of gravity* — the point where the weight is equal from all sides — is right in the center. The cone, however, is bigger at the bottom than it is at the top. When you balanced the pencil and eraser (see page 48), you saw how an object's center of gravity shifts toward the heavier part of the object; in the case of the cone, that's the bottom of it. So the center of gravity of a cone shape is lower — just as the TOWER-BUILDER'S CHECKLIST on pages 46 to 47 recommends! The heavier bottom helps the structure stand upright.

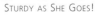

Round and Round We Go!

Most lighthouses are round in overall shape. That is so less of their surface is hit by water and wind.

In this diagram, the arrows represent the wind. How much of the surface of a flat object does the wind hit? All of it, and all at the same time! Now how much of the surface of a round object does the wind hit? Eventually all of it, but not all at the same time. Only a fraction of the circular structure is hit at once — the most prominent curve facing the sea. The circular shape makes the lighthouse more "wind resistant" than a flat surface.

It's true that some lighthouses are square or shaped like a pyramid without the top. What locations do you think these structures might be best designed for?

Start with a Sturdy Base!

Look again at the illustration of Cape Hatteras Light on page 40. Notice the wide base, clearly distinguishable from the rest of the structure, a style typical for conical tower lighthouses. To support that wide base, and the structure above it, the lighthouse must have an adequate foundation, just like a house or other large building. For added stability, part of a foundation is usually in the ground. The depth of the hole in which the foundation is built depends on the type of sand or soil in that particular location.

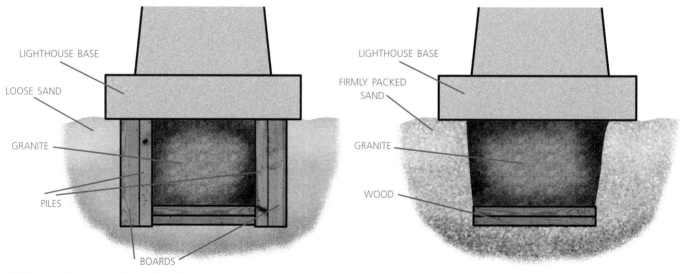

If the sand is loose, *piles* (weight-bearing support columns) are driven into the sand. Boards are placed vertically along the diameter of the hole, then granite is added. The base is built on top of this pile-wood-granite structure, which helps to anchor the base to the ground.

On more firmly packed sand, piles are not needed. Instead, wood and granite are placed in the ground, and the packed sand, combined with the wood and granite, form a solid foundation for the base.

Compare sand and soil

What you need

- ⚓ 2 empty plastic containers (like margarine tubs)
- ⚓ Sand
- ⚓ Potting or garden soil
- ⚓ 2 crayons

Which is better for a lighthouse tower's foundation — loose sand or firm soil? Fill one container about halfway with dry sand, and the other with packed soil. Stick an upright crayon in each container. Which one remains upright more easily? If you apply some force to your container, like a mini-earthquake, which crayon falls over more quickly? Experiment with adding more sand until you can get the crayon to stand securely. Can you see which material would work better for a lighthouse building site?

Still Lighting the Way!

Cape Hinchinbrook Lighthouse, Alaska

Built as an octagonal tower in 1910, no one thought anything could bring down this lighthouse in Alaska, and the builders declared it to be "earthquake proof." Unfortunately, they were wrong! Very intense quakes in 1927 and 1928 weakened the foundation and proved too much for the structure. It had to be rebuilt.

Today, this lighthouse looks like a tall rectangle, with elaborate designs on its sides. It is still standing — and shining! — at the entrance to Prince William Sound.

Tragedy on Minots Ledge

The story of the Minots Ledge Light is a reminder of how the careful design and construction of a lighthouse was crucial to its success and safety.

One of the most dangerous reefs on the East Coast is Minots Ledge, off the coast of Massachusetts (see page 11). The Minots Ledge reef is out in the ocean, so engineers weren't certain how to place a lighthouse on it. In the 1840s, an engineer named I.W.P. Lewis came up with the design of a combination screw-pile and skeleton (see page 67) lighthouse. He reasoned that the rough seas would flow through the skeletal structure, which would be secured to the ledge with thick iron piles screwed into the rock.

Many people thought the idea of placing the lighthouse on iron legs wouldn't work, but because about 40 ships had already struck the ledge and sunk, everyone agreed something must be done. So building began, and the original tower was lit for the first time on January 1, 1850.

For one year, the lighthouse did, indeed, live up to its expectations. And then a fierce hurricane ripped through the area. John Bennett, the lighthouse keeper at the time, had gone ashore, leaving behind his two assistants. He could only watch in horror as night fell and the seas and wind raged. Eventually, the light of the lighthouse went out. Even the bell rang no more. When morning came, the only things left of the Minots Ledge Light were a few spindly iron spikes poking up from the water. The two assistants died in the storm.

As a replacement light, it was decided that only a conical granite tower would do. The task was enormous, for the workers had to drill away the rock below the water in order to make the base. It took five years and cost $330,000, but in 1860, the new light was finally complete. It was made with more than 1,000 heavy granite bricks, totaling nearly 6,000 tons (5443 t) — about the weight of 1,500 elephants!

The original Minots Ledge Light was destroyed in a storm a year after it was built.

Minots Ledge Light, Massachusetts

The construction of the second Minots Ledge Light lived up to its expectations. It still stands today, guiding ships around the dangerous reef below. The tower is 114 feet (35 m), and the light can be seen for 15 miles (24 km).

Minots Ledge Light has a very distinctive beacon. Its light flashes one time, then four times, then three times. These are the same number of letters in each of the three words in "I love you"— 1, 4, and 3. So sometimes, people call this lighthouse the "I Love You" light!

THINK ABOUT IT!

Imagine how John Bennett must have felt during the storm, watching the lighthouse that was in his charge get swept away! Do you think he wanted to return to his job as keeper? If you could interview Bennett about the experience, what other questions would you ask him?

Make a lighthouse lamp!

Now it's *your* turn to create a tower lighthouse — one that really lights up! Here we show a conical tower with stripes, but your lighthouse might be square or rectangular and have a different pattern.

You will need adult supervision to make and use this light. Otherwise, enjoy making an unlit model of any of the lighthouses in the book (see pages 41 and 66 for good ideas and interesting shapes).

What you need

⚓ Gray crayon
⚓ Construction paper in gray, white, and red or black
⚓ Small sturdy cardboard box
⚓ Electric window candle
⚓ Packing tape
⚓ Ruler

⚓ For the lighthouse tower: white poster board or a square or rectangular cardboard box that's the height of the candlestick
⚓ Scissors
⚓ Glue
⚓ Paintbrush
⚓ Tempera paint, red or black
⚓ Paper or translucent plastic cup

What you do

1. To make the stone base for the lighthouse, use the crayon to decorate the construction paper as shown. Use this paper to cover the box.

2. Center the electric candle on the box; use the packing tape to secure it.

3. To make a cone-shaped tower, measure the height of your electric candle. Cut out the white poster board the same height. Roll it into a cone shape so that it fits easily around the light and on your small box. Then, holding its shape, remove it carefully, and glue the overlapping edges. Press firmly and let dry. Trim the bottom edges so it sits flat; trim the top evenly, too.

4. Cut out a small opening in the back of the tower for the light's cord. Center the tower around the light and glue it to the base. Place a lightweight object on top of the tower while the glue dries.

5. Choose an exterior design for your lighthouse tower. Paint the pattern on the tower; let dry.

6. Cut out a circle of red or black construction paper that's a little bigger than the top of the tower. Cut a circle in the center for the candle bulb to fit through, **making sure the opening is large enough so the paper is well away from the bulb.** Spread a line of glue along the top edge of the tower and gently press the paper circle in place; let dry.

7. Be sure the cup is large enough to sit over the light without being too close to the bulb. Sketch 4 evenly spaced "windows" on the cup and cut out. (With adult help, poke a hole in the cup to start each window.) Spread glue on the bottom of the cup and center it on the paper circle. Press it gently in place; let dry. Paint it black or red. (Use two coats of paint on a translucent cup.)

8. Cut out a small circle of black or red construction paper. Cut a slit to the center, then make a shallow cone shape as shown by overlapping the edges. Glue and press to hold; let dry. Glue it to the top of the cup. Plug in the candle, and turn on your lighthouse!*

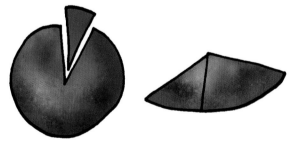

*Please don't leave your lamp unattended; be sure to turn it off when you leave the room.

Sambro Island Lighthouse, Nova Scotia, Canada — Oldest Original Lighthouse in North America!

Obviously this tower lighthouse was built to be super solid and strong, because it has guarded the south entrance to Halifax Harbor for almost 250 years! The original stone tower is covered with wooden shingles so the mortar won't deteriorate in the salt air. When first built, the tower was white. In 1908, the three red stripes were added, so the lighthouse would be more visible during the snowy winters on the Nova Scotia coast.

Lighthouse Legends & Lore

Like many lighthouses, Owls Head Lighthouse on the coast of Maine is said to be haunted by a former keeper. As the legend goes, people have heard doors slamming, windows shaking, and silverware rattling. The old keeper is a thrifty soul (he turns the thermostats down) and thoughtfully polishes the brass on the Fresnel lens from time to time!

CHAPTER 5

Offshore Lights

* Screw Piles, Caissons, Skeleton Lights & More! *

Towers standing tall on the shoreline might be the most familiar style of lighthouse, but they are not the only type you'll find. Many tower lights were built so tall because they are on low-lying coastal land, and their lights need to stretch as far as possible out across the ocean. Not all lighthouses serve this purpose, however. Lighthouses are designed to suit the land and the water around them. They're also built to warn mariners of specific navigational hazards in the area. So some lighthouses work most effectively when they are built right out in the water! A type called a wave-swept tower, for example, was built on rocky ledges offshore, warning mariners of these hazardous spots. And some locations don't require a tall lighthouse. One that's intended to guide ships in and out of a busy harbor, for example, doesn't need to be 100 feet (31 m) tall. Let's take a closer look at different styles of offshore lighthouses, and discover where they work best.

Supported by sturdy steel columns, a screw-pile lighthouse is an example of a style of lighthouse that sits right out in the water.

Screw-Pile Lighthouses

A screw-pile lighthouse was built right out in the water. Placed on top of sandy or rocky areas in shallow water, it alerted mariners to these hazardous locations. If you picture what a screw looks like, the name of this lighthouse will give you a clue as to what holds it in place. A *pile* is a long narrow column, often of steel, that's used for support; in this case, the piles have raised metal ridges called *threads* on the bottom, just like a screw does. These giant screws were sunk directly into the seafloor. The thick screw piles anchored the lighthouse in place.

How secure is a screw?

What you need

- ⚓ Hammer
- ⚓ Screwdriver
- ⚓ Nail and screw of roughly the same size
- ⚓ Block of scrap wood

With an adult's help, sink the nail and the screw partway into the block of scrap wood. Now, use the hammer as shown to try to remove them. Can you get them both out? With a little effort, you can pull the smooth nail back out, but the threads on the screw hold it in place. Screw piles were an important engineering device to keep these lighthouses securely anchored to the ocean floor.

Ice Floe, Straight Ahead!

At one time, screw-pile lighthouses were very popular in the United States. The U.S. government liked building them because they didn't cost a lot of money (much less than a tall tower lighthouse). Relatively quick and easy to build, screw piles were often used to replace lightships (see page 67). By the late 1800s, about 100 screw-pile lighthouses had been built in the United States. Today, not many are left. Turns out they weren't as sturdy as people thought!

The biggest danger to screw-pile lighthouses were ice floes. These huge flat masses of sea ice often don't float on by. If they get caught on the base of a screw-pile light, they will stay there, and the motion of the water moves the ice floe up and down against the screw piles. It's only a matter of time before the piles are weakened and come tumbling down.

Where do you think screw-pile lighthouses were *not* built? If you said up north, you're right! Most screw-pile lights were along the mid-Atlantic coast and down into Florida, where ice floes were not a problem.

Crunch!

⚡TRY IT!⚡ Make a mini ice floe

Fill a sink or plastic tub with water and put in some ice cubes. Move your hands in the water to form a water current. Where do the ice cubes end up? The current moves them in one direction until they bump the edge of the sink or tub. What happens as the ripples of water keep moving the ice cubes? The ice cubes continue to beat against the side, just the way the ice floes beat against the "legs" of a screw-pile lighthouse.

Do you think a lighthouse could have saved the *Titanic*, which sank in the North Sea in 1912 when it hit an iceberg, killing hundreds of people? It is possible, but unlikely, that a lighthouse would have helped. Unfortunately, no lighthouses have ever been built in the middle of the ocean. The ocean is much too deep for that. Also, the bottom of an iceberg — the part below the water's surface — is much bigger than the part of the iceberg we see above the water. So a lighthouse wouldn't be able to tell a ship's captain exactly how big the iceberg was and how close the ship could pass.

Learn the Lingo!

peninsula: a portion of land that juts out from the shore into the water; often nearly surrounded by water

shoal: a ridge of sand that creates a shallow area in the water

The Chesapeake Bay

One of the most popular places for screw-pile lighthouses has been the Chesapeake Bay, on the shores of Maryland and Virginia. Take a look at the map on this page. What do you notice about the bay? It has dozens of tiny inlets and peninsulas — and that's just what you can see above the water! It also has rocky reefs and shoals, and you've seen what a hazard to ships those can be. Screw-pile lighthouses, then, became the lighthouse of choice. Between 1850 and 1900, 42 screw-pile lighthouses were built along the Chesapeake Bay — more than anywhere else in the world!

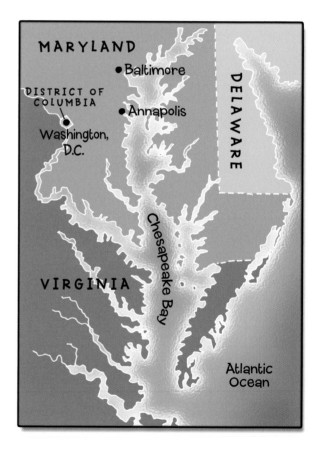

Thomas Point Shoal Light, Maryland

Thomas Point Shoal Light is one of the last cottage-style screw-pile lighthouses still in operation in the United States. It sits at the mouth of the South River, south of Annapolis, Maryland. (Can you find this location on the map on page 60?) It was built in 1875 to replace a lighthouse located on the nearby shore that was ineffective because of its location.

In 1972, the United States Coast Guard (see page 86) thought it best to take apart the house, or cottage, that sat on the screw piles. The citizens of Maryland protested, and the lighthouse was saved. Today, the Thomas Point Shoal Lighthouse is one of 10 lighthouses that have been designated a National Historic Landmark. With this designation, the lighthouse has been preserved for generations to come.

The Thomas Point Shoal Light is currently not open to visitors, but people are working on it. A dock has been constructed beside the lighthouse, and eventually you'll be able to take a guided boat tour to visit it. The lighthouse cottage is not very big, so only small groups of about 15 to 25 people will be allowed there at one time.

If Not by Sea, Then by Land!

The Thomas Point Shoal Light is the only screw-pile lighthouse still in its original location, but that doesn't mean you can't visit a few others. The cottages of several screw-pile lighthouses have been removed and restored on land, where they are now museums (see RESOURCES, page 92).

Make a screw-pile lighthouse!

Use your screw-pile model to explain to others about these special lighthouses and how they were used!

What you need

- ⚓ Single-serving cereal box
- ⚓ White paper
- ⚓ Scissors
- ⚓ Glue
- ⚓ Paper-towel tube
- ⚓ Red paper
- ⚓ Sharp pencil
- ⚓ Tape
- ⚓ Dark marker
- ⚓ 16 pipe cleaners

What you do

1. Cover the bottom and sides of the box with white paper, and glue it in place.

2. Open up the "doors" of the small cereal box. This will actually be the roof of your lighthouse. Place the cardboard tube through the doors, so it sticks up in the middle as shown. Cut the tube so that about 2" (5 cm) show above the doors.

3. Remove the tube and glue red paper around it. Place the tube back inside the doors and glue it in place.

4. Center your house upside down on a piece of red construction paper and trace around the tube as shown. Cut out the hole and slide the paper down the tube. Glue the paper to the box so that it covers the openings on both sides of the tube and the slanted roof sections (trim the paper as necessary). Tape down any edges as needed.

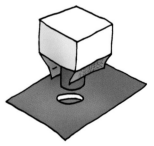

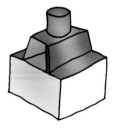

Cover the remainder of the "roof" with red paper.

This is your lighthouse cottage. Draw on windows and any other decorative features that you want.

5. With the sharp pencil point, poke eight holes in the bottom of the box, as shown.

6. Twist two pipe cleaners together as shown.

Repeat with the other seven pairs. Now place the pipe cleaners into the holes so they dangle down. These are the screw piles of your lighthouse. Bend the ends of each pair so the "piles" support your lighthouse.

TRY IT! 🏃 Choose a state symbol

The Thomas Point Shoal Light is often shown as a symbol of Maryland and the Chesapeake Bay. You can see it on postcards, on books about Maryland, even on billboards. And it was almost used as Maryland's emblem on the back of the Maryland state quarter!

What would be a good symbol for your state? Do you live in a state that has lighthouses? Do you have other historical buildings or places where an important historical event occurred that would make good symbols? Draw your own postcard or mini-billboard — or even state quarter! — with the state symbol *you* would choose.

"... the shoal, below about 1 foot [30 cm] of soft mud and shell, was found to consist of hard blue sand and shell, with a slight trace of mud to a depth of 20 feet [6 m]. It is believed that a secure foundation can be had at a depth of 12 feet [3.5 m] or less. ...

The tube will be of the form ... of a cone .... The shell will be built up in sections, bolted together ... and sunk in position by filling it with concrete. It will be protected on the outside from the scour of the tide by ... loose stone. The keeper's dwelling will rest on this solid structure."

—from the annual report of the U.S. Lighthouse Board, 1873, regarding construction of the Thomas Point Shoal Light

THINK ABOUT IT!

Which U.S. state has the most lighthouses? Before you decide, look at the map on pages 90 to 91 and think about large bodies of water in the United States. Then see the answer below.

The state of Michigan has more lighthouses than any other state! Are you surprised? The shores of the Great Lakes are dotted with lighthouses. To learn more about them, see RESOURCES, page 92.

The Caisson Light

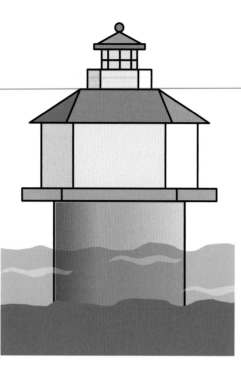

In addition to being prone to ice damage, screw-pile lighthouses could be fragile during bad weather (see the story of the Minots Ledge Light, pages 52 to 53), so another lighthouse style was designed for lighthouses that stand in the water. These lighthouses were called caisson lights. Instead of screw piles that anchored the lighthouse structure to the sea floor, a *caisson* (a large watertight iron cylinder) was sunk into the seafloor. The lighthouse with its light was then placed on top of the iron tube.

Make a mini caisson light

What you need

⚓ Your screw-pile lighthouse model (see pages 62 to 63)
⚓ Sturdy paper (thick construction paper, card stock, or an old file folder)
⚓ Tape

Turn your screw-pile lighthouse into a caisson light to see why this type of lighthouse was sturdier. Remove the pipe-cleaner legs from your model. Roll the sturdy paper into a big tube and tape the edges together. Stand the tube on end, then tape the cottage on top. One end of the tube would be securely wedged into the seafloor, while the other end supported the lighthouse!

People came up with several fancy names for these types of lighthouses to describe their stout little shapes — teakettle lighthouse, coffeepot lighthouse, even spark-plug lighthouse! What will you call yours?

Duxbury Pier Lighthouse, Massachusetts

The first cast-iron caisson light built in the U.S., Duxbury Pier Light marks a dangerous shoal outside of Plymouth Harbor. Shaped a bit like a coffeepot, this stubby little light is known locally as "Bug Light" or simply "the Bug." During a huge hurricane in 1944, this remote offshore lighthouse was pounded with 30-foot (9-m) waves, but it held fast (well, it did shake a little!), thanks in part to the 100 tons (91 t) of stone placed around its base.

"The gigantic waves were hammering this stout little light station unmercifully. It shook so bad we had trouble keeping the oil lamps lit … The heavy seas on the east side were striking against the light, then crashing up under the catwalk and tearing away at our boat that we had previously lashed high."

—Harry Salter, lighthouse keeper at Duxbury Pier Light during the hurricane of 1944

Lighthouse Legends & Lore

The legend of this lighthouse involves pirates! The Boca Grande Light sits on the island of Gasparilla, off the west coast of Florida in the Gulf of Mexico. The island was once owned by a fierce pirate named José Gaspar. Legend has it that Gaspar attacked more than 400 ships in his day. He was also rumored to have buried treasure along the west coast of Florida, which has never been found.

Many years before the lighthouse was built in 1809, Gaspar used Gasparilla as his retreat. He often stayed here to rest and recuperate after plundering ships at sea. People visiting the the Boca Grande Light claim to see the ghost of a woman walking the beaches, supposedly a Spanish princess who became one of Gaspar's victims after she refused his offer of marriage.

ARRR!*

*Pirate-speak for "what's up?"

Even More Lighthouse Styles!

Here are some other types of lighthouse designs for offshore locations.
See if you can match the illustrations with the names on page 67.

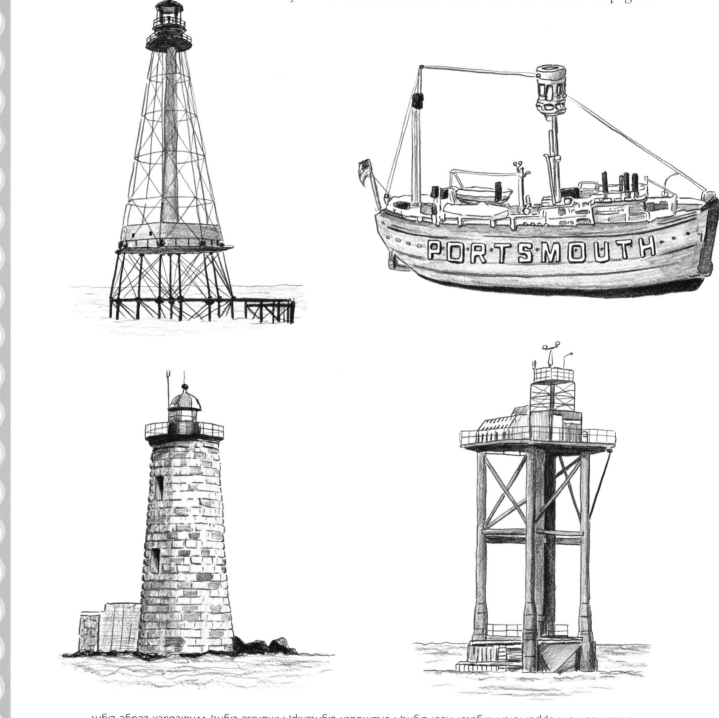

Clockwise from upper left: Alligator Reef Light, *Portsmouth* Lightship, Ambrose Light, Whaleback Ledge Light

Skeleton Light Tower

These lights are built out in the water. You can frequently find skeleton lights in Florida, where they alert mariners to rocky shoals and reefs.

Shown on the facing page is Alligator Reef Light, off the tip of Florida, which warns ships of a jagged coral reef that has been responsible for many shipwrecks.

Lightship

A lightship is a floating lighthouse! Typically, these ships would anchor at a strategic location at sea and remain there for months at a time. Although it might seem like a good idea — place a light on a boat, and the crew of the boat can maintain the light — lightships were very dangerous for the crew members. Beside the risk from bad seas and foul weather, lightships were also in danger of being hit by the ships they were trying to help, especially in heavy fog. Because of the danger, lightships were mostly replaced by skeleton lights or Texas towers.

Shown on the facing page is the lightship *Portsmouth*, which served for 48 years off the coasts of Virginia, Delaware, and Massachusetts.

Texas Tower

This lighthouse looks like an oil rig! And in fact, the design is based on the offshore oil-drilling platforms that you might see in the Gulf Coast region of Texas and Louisiana.

Shown on the facing page is the original Ambrose Light, located off the coasts of New York and New Jersey. When this tower was replaced, large sections of the new lighthouse were assembled in Virginia and brought to the site out in the ocean on a barge.

Wave-Swept Tower

This type of lighthouse is built on a large piece of rock in the middle of the water. The most famous wave-swept tower is the Eddystone Light in England, but there are some in North America, too!

Shown on the facing page is a wave-swept tower off the coast of New England. Although officially located in the waters of Maine, Whaleback Ledge Light guards the entrance to the harbor of the city of Portsmouth, New Hampshire. Can you find the other wave-swept towers in this book?

Dubh Artach Light (page 48), Minots Ledge Light (page 53), and St. George Reef Light (page 68) are also wave-swept towers.

Shine a Light On ...

ST. GEORGE REEF LIGHT, CALIFORNIA —
America's Most Expensive Lighthouse!

Built on tiny Seal Rock, 6 miles (9.5 km) off the coast of California near the Oregon border, the wave-swept tower called St. George Reef Light was one of the most exposed lighthouses constructed on the West Coast. It cost more than $700,000 to build this small tower, and so it also has the reputation of being the most expensive lighthouse ever built in the U.S. What's more, it was considered one of the most dangerous stations in lighthouse history; during its many years of service, four keepers were killed while on duty.

Located a mere 17 feet (5.2 m) above sea level, the lighthouse offered no safe landing area for boats. At one time, a large boom was used to "swing" personnel and supplies over from the deck of a ship designed specifically to service off-shore lighthouses, called a *lighthouse tender*.

The St. George Reef Light was deactivated in 1975, and is now maintained by a preservation society. Tours are available — and public access is by helicopter!

> "St. George Reef Lighthouse represents one of the greatest challenges in U.S. lighthouse building history. Besides being one of the most expensive ever built at that time, it took eight years to complete."
> —Historic Light Station Information, U.S. Coast Guard

The Wreck of the "Brother Jonathan"

In 1865, the passenger steamer *Brother Jonathan* crashed on St. George Reef, resulting in many lost lives. The ship was so overloaded with passengers and cargo that at first the captain refused to head out, but he ultimately yielded to orders from the ship's owners.

The *Brother Jonathan* headed out of San Francisco Bay, where it quickly encountered severe winds and rough seas. The steamer then attempted to reach the Crescent City harbor, which required passing through the treacherous St. George Reef. During humid weather, the reef "smokes" — it produces a thick, smokelike spray that obscures the rocks. With limited visibility, the ship struck the reef at 2 P.M., on Sunday, July 30. A lifeboat with 19 occupants arrived at the Crescent City Lighthouse at about 5 P.M. that day. They were the only survivors. Accounts vary, but at least 166 people had drowned. Plans for the construction of a lighthouse began soon afterward.

THINK ABOUT IT!

Before you turn the page, think about the word *lighthouse*. *Lighthouse* is, of course, a compound word — *light* and *house*. But so far, you've seen tall towers of stone, cottages perched on screw piles, and skeleton lights. What do you think a lighthouse might look like, if it truly captured the meaning of the word? Draw what you imagine, then turn the page.

TRY IT! Take the design challenge!

In this chapter and the previous one, you've seen some of the problems lighthouse engineers faced. Try your hand at solving them! What do you think would be good designs for lighthouses in the following situations? Consider the different features each lighthouse will need to be successful in its location, and draw a sketch of your design.

* *Challenge:* This lighthouse will stand on a low-lying section of marshy shoreline, where a large river flows into the sea.

* *Challenge:* This lighthouse will sit on a rocky ledge where two fast-flowing currents meet. Heavy storms are frequent in winter and occasional ice floes pass through the area.

* *Challenge:* This lighthouse will be located in an area where heavy fogs roll in quickly. It will be near another lighthouse on a very similar-looking curve of coastline.

House + Light = Lighthouse!

Your drawing (see THINK ABOUT IT!, page 69) might look a bit like the lighthouse below. That's because it is what the name implies — simply a house with a light! Many of these lighthouses are found along the Great Lakes and the Pacific Coast. Because the lighthouse might sit atop a cliff, the tower does not need to be so tall. The base, then, can simply be the house!

Still Lighting the Way!

East Brother Island Lighthouse, California

If you looked at this house quickly, you might not even notice the light at first — it looks as if it is part of the house! The lighthouse tower is actually a separate structure, and the house is built right alongside it. This lighthouse is near Richmond, California, and it was built in 1874. Not only has East Brother Lighthouse been functional for more than 130 years, but also people can actually stay in this lighthouse — it's now a bed-and-breakfast!

TRY IT! Wish you were here!

Imagine you are staying at the East Brother Island Lighthouse. It is situated on East Brother Island at the tip of Point San Pablo, off the coast of California near San Francisco. Make a postcard to tell someone back home about it. On the blank side of a large index card, draw a picture of the lighthouse. On the lined side of the card, write about your visit. Describe the sights, sounds, and smells of the Pacific shoreline.

CHAPTER 6

Keepers of the Flame!

✳ Lighthouse Keepers & Their Families ✳

So now you know a lot about the best locations for lighthouses, different styles of lighthouses and how they're constructed, and what makes those huge lights so bright. But there is one other part of the lighthouse story that you're probably especially curious about — the people who lived inside! Some lighthouse keepers lived alone; others brought their families. Although you might imagine days of peaceful solitude, a keeper's life was fraught with danger, especially if a storm raged at sea!

Nowadays all the remaining active lighthouses in the U.S. have automated lights, so the days of the lighthouse keeper climbing the tower to light the lamp are long gone. Let's step back in time to meet some of these courageous people and learn what the job of tending the coasts, day and night, rain or shine, was like.

THINK ABOUT IT!

One part of the poem you might be wondering about is the line "and their trash drops in the ocean." Dumping your garbage into the sea to get rid of it might seem like an outdated attitude — but it is a huge problem! Hundreds of pounds of trash are left on public beaches every year. This trash, along with garbage dropped overboard by careless boaters, is often consumed by marine animals, who sicken and die. So be sure to pick up after yourselves before you leave a public beach, lake, or waterfront park. Your water-dwelling friends will thank you for keeping them healthy and safe!

A Poet's Inspiration

This poem was recited by Captain Stetson Turner, whose father was a lighthouse keeper in Maine in the 1930s. This poem paints the life of a lighthouse keeper as one that is not very difficult and is rather pleasant — no noisy neighbors, such complete privacy that you don't need to draw the curtains to undress, and plenty of exercise from climbing all those stairs!

Although the poem does convey an idyllic life, the light keeper's life could be quite dangerous at times. What do you think about the image of lighthouse life the poem portrays? Does it seem realistic? What parts of it are appealing to you?

Lighthouse Keepers

Lighthouse keepers have it easy
All year long their homes are breezy;
Noises don't disturb their labors,
For they haven't any neighbors.

They don't need big wastebaskets
For old papers, orange peels, or gaskets;
Just one careless motion
And their trash drops in the ocean.

They don't need nine holes or twenty,
They get exercise aplenty;
One trip up the spiral stairway
Equals three around the fairway.

Window shades are never needed,
They can dress or strip unheeded;
Wakeful brats don't have conniptions,
Neighbors don't give long descriptions.

When I'm old and don't need pity,
I shall leave the sullied city,
Climb a lighthouse, bar the door,
And trim my wicks forevermore.

Author Unknown

Interview with a Lighthouse Keeper!

The job of lighthouse keeper was very different from the work most people in a community do. If you had the opportunity to ask longtime keeper Joshua Strout a few questions about his job, here's how he might answer.

Did you go to a lighthouse keeper's training school?

I didn't have any formal training for my job, but I did have a set of instructions to follow (see page 74). Written in 1835, these instructions were the first to spell out exactly what the lighthouse keepers should do — even though the first lighthouse in America had been built around 1762! For those first 100 years, when lighthouses were under the supervision of the U.S. Treasury Department, lighthouse keepers had to kind of "wing it"!

Joshua Strout was the keeper of the Portland Head Lighthouse (see page 22) from 1869 to 1904.

How did you get hired?

In 1852, the newly formed U.S. Lighthouse Board (see page 86) listed requirements for lighthouse keepers:

★ We had to be between 18 and 50 years old.

★ We had to be able to read, write, and "keep accounts," or know math.

★ We had to be physically able to do manual labor and to pull and sail a boat.

★ We also had to know enough about mechanics to be able to make minor repairs.

I met all those requirements, so I got the job!

People chosen to be lighthouse keepers were then put on "probation" for three months. If the supervisors thought the keeper did a good enough job during that period, the temporary keeper received the position permanently. I held my post for 35 years!

Did you earn a salary?

Yes, about $600 a year! (That would be about $13,000 in today's money value.) Divide that by 52 to find out how much I earned a week!

Did you get sick days or vacations?

Not really. If I wanted to take a day off, I had to get permission first.

The Keeper's "Assistant"

Even the Strout family's parrot Billy had a job. When a thick fog rolled into the area, he would announce, "It's foggy! It's foggy! Start the horn!" If you were a lighthouse keeper with a pet parrot, what phrases would you teach it?

(73)

Here is a partial list of the instructions that Steven Pleasonton, in charge of U.S. lighthouses from 1820 to 1852, wrote detailing the job of keeper. After reading this list of instructions, which do you think would be the hardest instruction to follow regularly? Which would be the easiest? Would you like the job of keeper?

Instructions to the Keepers of Light Houses within the United States

- You are to light the lamps every evening at sun-setting, and keep them continually burning, bright and clear, till sun-rising.

- You are to be careful that the lamps, reflectors, and lanterns are constantly kept clean, and in order; and particularly to be careful that no lamps, wood, or candles be left burning anywhere as to endanger fire.

- In order to maintain the greatest degree of light during the night, the wicks are to be trimmed every four hours, taking care that they are exactly even on the top.

- You are to keep an exact amount of the quantity of oil received from time to time; the number of gallons, quarts, gills [4 fluid ounces/113 grams] consumed each night; and deliver a copy of the same to the Superintendent every three months, ending 31 March, 30 June, 30 September, and 31 December, in each year; with an account of the quantity on hand at the time.

- You will not be absent yourself from the Light-house at any time, without first obtaining the consent of the Superintendent, unless the occasion be so sudden and urgent as not to admit of an application to that officer; in which case, by leaving a suitable substitute, you may be absent for twenty-four hours.

Were Lighthouse Keepers Always Men?

The guidelines put out by the Lighthouse Board stated that lighthouse keepers had to be physically able to do manual labor and sail a boat. Lighthouse keepers also had to read, write, and be able to do math. At the time when lighthouses were staffed with keepers, many women had not been taught these skills. In fact, during the 1800s, many people did not think it was appropriate for women to do strenuous physical labor, as a man would. So right away, women would not be considered good candidates to run a lighthouse. However, as Ida Lewis and Abbie Burgess (see page 80) proved, women could, indeed, be excellent lighthouse keepers!

Spotlight on Ida Lewis

Ida Lewis was perhaps one of the most famous female lighthouse operators ever! Born in 1842, she and her family lived at the Lime Rock Lighthouse in Rhode Island, on a small rocky ledge only about 650 feet (200 m) from shore. Ida didn't have time to go to school herself, but every day she rowed her younger siblings back and forth to the mainland so they could go to school. At that time, it was not considered proper for a woman to handle a boat, but Ida proved that a young woman could be quite competent at these tasks! With these skills, Ida performed many daring rescues during her lifetime, and her bravery became front-page news.

    Although Ida's mother became the official lighthouse keeper in 1879 after Ida's father died, Ida remained at the job. Eventually Ida became the official keeper until her death in 1911. In 1924, the lighthouse was renamed Ida Lewis Rock Light in her honor. It was deactivated in 1963.

Lighthouse keeper Ida Lewis became nationally famous for all the daring rescues she performed.

Light Keepers and Their Families

Sometimes lighthouse keepers lived alone in the lighthouse, but often a married couple with children would all live together in the keeper's house. The residence was not much different from a regular house you might find in a neighborhood — only its closest neighbor was the lighthouse! Although the life might seem harsh and lonely, accounts by lighthouse keepers and their families described the experience as rather wonderful.

"From the first, the work had a fascination for me. I loved the water, having always been near it, and I loved to stand in the tower and watch the great rolling waves chasing and tumbling in upon the shore. It was hard to tell when it was loveliest. Whether in its quiet moods or in a raging foam."

—Elizabeth Williams, keeper of the Beaver Island Harbor Point Light (1872–1884) and Little Traverse Light Station (1884–1913) in Michigan

TRY IT! Turn your home into a lighthouse residence!

What would your home look like with a lighthouse attached? Draw a picture of your house — then add a tower lighthouse to the picture! What would you see from the top of the tower?

It's a Long Way to the Grocery Store!

Lighthouse keepers and their families could not make a quick hop to the local store for supplies. Like early settlers and pioneers, most keepers were very self-reliant. They hunted waterfowl (or birds) for meat, and they fished the waters for seafood. If there was enough soil, lighthouse families also grew gardens of vegetables. They might even have a cow for milk or chickens for fresh eggs!

⚝TRY IT!⚝ Make a lighthouse menu

It's dinnertime at the lighthouse. Before the sun sets and your family must prepare for the night's activities, you all sit down to supper. Think of a healthy meal a lighthouse family might eat, using only seafood and fresh vegetables, and prepare a dinner menu for them. Do you eat a similar dish at home with these foods? Would you enjoy eating this dinner?

Take a Hike!

Families that lived at the Point Sur Lighthouse, near Big Sur, California, didn't have to take a boat to their homes. But that doesn't mean getting there was easy! They had to hike up a cliff, more than 200 feet (60 m) tall! Typically, four families lived at the top of this cliff. The cliff was so difficult to get up and down from that the families rarely left their Pacific perch. Instead, supplies were hoisted up to the families by cranes! Even soil for farming had to be brought up the hill because the soil at the top was not rich enough for growing vegetables.

Time for School!

Going to school was difficult for children who lived at a lighthouse, but they still had to get an education. Here are a few inventive ways their parents got them to school:

* If the lighthouse was on an island, the parent would row the children to the mainland and they would then walk to the local school.

* Parents would trade off with another family during the year; one family lived on the mainland or in town so the kids could go to school, while another family lived at the lighthouse. Then they'd switch. Sometimes the teacher would come out to the lighthouse to teach the kids!

"The island is made up of nothing but rocks, without one foot of ground for trees, shrubs, or grass. The broad Atlantic lies before and all around us. Now and then sails dot the wide expanse, reminding me that there is a world besides the little one I dwell in, all surrounded by water.

"After school-hours, I turn my eyes and thoughts toward the mainland and think how I should like to be there, and enjoy some of those delightful sleigh-rides which I am deprived of while shut out here from the world."

—Annie Bell Hobbs, about 14, daughter of the keeper of the Boon Island Light Station in Maine, 1876

THINK ABOUT IT!

It might seem cool to miss school because you had to live far away at a lighthouse with your family, but you might miss a few things too! Think about aspects of your school — and your school life — that you really like. Make a list of the things you would miss if you could not go to school, but instead lived most of your life at a lighthouse, alone with your family. Or, perhaps you are home-schooled or have friends who are. What might you or your friends have in common with lighthouse kids?

☆TRY IT!☆ Step into the shoes of a lighthouse kid!

Here are some things you would have experienced as a lighthouse kid long ago.
Do any describe your life today?

A lighthouse kid …

★ Lived near the water all year long.

★ Stayed with his or her family nearly all the time.

★ Had lots of long evenings filled with reading and other quiet activities.

★ Didn't always go to school with other children (but sometimes did; it depended how far away the lighthouse was from a town).

★ Was expected to help with chores around the house.

★ Didn't have stores or a mall nearby to shop frequently for clothes or other necessities.

★ Couldn't make a quick trip to the grocery store to buy food; tended vegetables in a garden, raised chickens for fresh eggs, and ate a lot of fresh seafood!

★ Didn't have a doctor, dentist, or hospital close by in case of an emergency.

★ Went boating and fishing often.

★ Only received mail when the family went ashore every few weeks for supplies.

★ Didn't have friends visit often, but when they did, it was probably for a sleepover!

Lighthouse Kids on the Job!

Living in a lighthouse was much like living on the frontier or out on the prairie, except that the families had a ready-made home, and they had an important job to do for the government. Their parents had the responsibility to watch the waters and maintain the lights, so children were often responsible for other daily chores, such as tending to the garden, keeping the home clean, and doing the laundry (without a washing machine, of course!). Kids also helped with fishing or hunting for food. At times, these lighthouse kids assisted their parents with the duties of keeper, and in emergencies, some had to care for the light, too!

Spotlight on Abbie Burgess

In 1853 when Abbie Burgess was 14 years old, her father became the keeper of the Matinicus Rock Light — more than 20 miles (32.2 km) off the coast of Maine! Abbie's father, Samuel Burgess, moved his entire family to the island, which included Abbie's brother, three younger sisters, and her mother, who could not walk. Abbie's brother, Benjy, often chose to go fishing rather than to stay at the lighthouse. Abbie, therefore, became an important assistant to her father, helping him take care of the lighthouse and learning how to light the lantern.

This experience all came in very handy when a storm stranded Abbie's father during a trip to shore to get supplies. In fact, the storm was so bad, that the waves were smashing against the keeper's house. Abbie had to help her mother and younger sisters get into one of the island's two lighthouse towers for safety. Even after the storm was over, the sea was so rough that no landing could be made on the island, so Abbie's father didn't return for *four weeks*! During that entire time, Abbie kept the light lit and cared for her family.

Chronicle the storm

What you need

⚓ Computer and CD or tape recorder   ⚓ Writing paper and pen

⚓ Flashlight or small camping lantern

Imagine you are 20 miles (32 km) out to sea, with the waves crashing against your house. You need to stay calm because your family — and the ships at sea! — are depending on you. Write a letter to a friend on the mainland, recording your thoughts and experiences during the storm.

     To get in the mood and imagine what it might have been like to be this lighthouse kid, make a sound-effects tape! Come up with clever ways to create howling wind and waves crashing against the rocks or even against the lighthouse itself and record the sounds, or search online for storm sounds to download to a CD. Then play your sounds as you write your letter. Use a flashlight or small camping lantern as a "candle" to light your desk. Then compare your letter with Abbie's own description below of her experience.

In Her Own Words ...

Here is a portion of a letter Abbie Burgess wrote to a friend about that big storm in January 1856.

> Father was away. Early in the day, as the tide arose, the sea made a complete breach over the rock, washing every movable thing away, and of the old dwelling not one stone was left upon another. The new dwelling was flooded, and the windows had to be secured to prevent the violence of the spray from breaking them in. As the tide came, the sea rose higher and higher, till the only endurable places were the light-towers. If they stood we were saved, otherwise our fate was all too certain ...
>
> For four weeks owing to rough weather, no landing could be effected on the rock ... Though at times greatly exhausted with my labors, not once did the lights fail ... I was able to perform all my accustomed duties as well as my father's.

SADDLEBACK LEDGE LIGHT, MAINE

If you look at the Saddleback Ledge Light today, all you'll see is a squattish brick tower perched on a rocky island off the coast of Maine. But until 1954, this lighthouse, once described as one of the most remote and barren of Maine's lighthouses, still had a lighthouse keeper.

One of the biggest challenges about living at this lighthouse was actually getting onto the island itself. The island is so rocky that a boat could not dock there properly. Instead, passengers had to be swung from the deck of the boat out over the water and onto the island in a specially

designed seat called a *bosun's chair*. In an interview for a book on lighthouse history, June Dudley Watts, daughter of the keeper Leonard Dudley, told the author that she was always relieved to be in her father's strong arms after the "hair-raising" ride in the chair.

> "It is a never-to-be-forgotten experience to be swung around and landed from the rocking deck of a small craft onto the hard rocky ledge, and those of us who have had that sensation do not forget it in a hurry."
> — historian Edward Rowe Snow

A 21-Day Vigil

A legendary lighthouse story involves a 15-year-old boy, the son of the keeper at lonely Saddleback Ledge Light. One day, the father went to the mainland to get supplies. Before he was able to head back, however, a huge storm came up. The storm lasted 21 days. Each night, the father watched anxiously from shore. If the light in the lighthouse tower came on, he knew his son was still okay. And each night for 21 nights, his son climbed the tower stairs and lit the lamp! Somehow, he was able to survive on his meager food supply, too.

♨ TRY IT! ♨ Write a fitting tribute

Look back at the poem about keepers on page 72. What do you think about a lighthouse keeper's life now after reading this chapter? Do you agree that "lighthouse keepers have it easy"? Write a new verse or two for the poem that reflects experiences of being a lighthouse keeper that the original poet did not describe.

Swap lighthouse stories!

What you need

⚓ Paper

⚓ Pencil

⚓ Three friends

Imagine that Ida Lewis (see page 75), Abbie Burgess (see page 80), the keeper's son from Saddleback Ledge Light (page 82), and Maebelle Mason (see below) met and shared their lighthouse experiences. What would they say to each other? Write a conversation between these courageous lighthouse residents. Have the characters compare their experiences, perhaps bragging about who survived harsher ordeals. Have fun performing this mini-play with your friends!

There She Rows!

Here's yet another tale of a heroic lighthouse keeper's child! Maebelle L. Mason lived with her family in a lighthouse along the Detroit River, which flows into Lake Erie. On May 11, 1890, Maebelle saw a rowboat carrying a man capsize. Her father, the lighthouse keeper, was away at the time, so 14-year-old Maebelle rowed for more than a mile (1.6 km) in the family boat, hauled the drowning man over the side, and rowed back to the station.

Make an honorary plaque

Make sure that the daring adventures and steadfast service of North America's many lighthouse keepers are not forgotten! Choose one of the keepers you have read about in this book to commemorate with a plaque. Perhaps you wish to record Joshua Strout's many years of service (see page 73), Abbie Burgess's responsible tending of her father's light (see page 80), or Martin Knudsen's brave rescue of shipwrecked passengers (see page 35). Now they are ready to be inducted into a Lighthouse Hall of Fame!

"It is not only the shipwrecked to whom Mrs. Norvell opened her doors. In every big hurricane or storm here since 1891, her lighthouse has been a refuge for fishermen and others whose homes have been swept away. In the … storm of 1903 Mrs. Norvell's lighthouse was the only building left standing on the lower coast, and over 200 survivors found a welcome and shelter in her home."

—from a newspaper article about Margaret Norvell, Louisiana lighthouse keeper from 1891–1932

What you need

⚓ Scissors
⚓ Dark-colored construction paper
⚓ Shoe-box lid
⚓ Glue
⚓ White paper
⚓ Scrap paper and pencil (optional)
⚓ Markers

What you do

1. Cut a piece of dark-colored construction paper to fit inside the shoe-box lid. Glue the paper to the lid.

2. Cut out a slightly smaller piece of white paper.

3. On the white paper, you'll write about the person you are honoring, but you might want to write a draft on scrap paper first. You might begin with words like, "This plaque is being awarded to _____ in recognition of _____ ." Continue writing about what makes this keeper special. Be sure to add the dates of service or of the event you are commemorating, too.

4. Visit the web sites for the various lighthouses (see RESOURCES, page 92) to look for photos and quotes to include on your plaque, if you like. Or decorate it with original artwork.

5. Copy the final version onto the white paper. Center it on the dark-colored construction paper inside the lid and glue it in place.

CHAPTER 7

Lighthouses Today

* Links to the Past That Still Light the Way! *

The operation of lighthouses has changed quite a bit since the Boston Light was first lit in 1716, followed by the light at the Fortress of Louisburg on Cape Breton Island in Canada about 20 years later. With the invention of sonar (see page 9), lighthouses are unnecessary in most locations. And although many lighthouses do still shine, the lamps of all U.S. lighthouses are now automated (they are set on a timer and go on and off automatically), so lighthouse keepers are not needed.

With most lighthouses no longer essential for safe navigation, today they serve a different purpose. These intriguing structures recall the early days of North America, when the United States and Canada were being explored and settled, and approaching the rugged coastlines in a sailing ship was often a dangerous undertaking. Lighthouses represent an era when sophisticated navigation equipment had yet to be invented and people relied on a simple flame to guide ships safely home. These coastal lights are links to our maritime history, and there is an active effort to preserve many of them as national landmarks.

Many lighthouses, whether operational or deactivated, are open to the public. Eager to take a tour? Turn to Resources on page 92 to discover lighthouses you can visit.

CLICK!

Who's in Charge of Lighthouses?

Over the decades, U.S. lighthouses have been overseen by various government agencies, including the U.S. Lighthouse Board and the U.S. Bureau of Lighthouses, also known as the Lighthouse Service. In 1939, President Franklin D. Roosevelt decided that America's lighthouses should fall under the jurisdiction of the U.S. Coast Guard (a branch of the Armed Forces), and that is where they remain today. Also overseen for many years by a Lighthouse Board, operational lighthouses on Canadian shores are now supervised by the Canadian Coast Guard. To date, about 50 lighthouses in Canada are still staffed by keepers.

Some North American lighthouses have been preserved as National Historic Landmarks or are under the care of the National Historic Sites of Canada, and some of these are still-functioning lights. See RESOURCES on page 92 for more information.

The Coast Guard Steps In

In the 1960s, the U.S. Coast Guard started LAMP — the Lighthouse Automation and Modernization Program. Its purpose was to update lighthouses and their equipment. Under the program, fewer and fewer lighthouses were deemed necessary. Their lights were put out forever, or the lighthouse structure was replaced by a floating buoy with a light. If the lighthouse was kept active, the light was automated.

Currently, a special unit of the U.S. Coast Guard called ANT — Aid to Navigation Team — is responsible for maintaining America's modern-day lighthouses. Sixty-four ANT units take care of about 400 still-working lights. Unlike lighthouse keepers of old, who spent every day caring for their lighthouses, an ANT unit makes only occasional visits to individual lighthouses throughout the year. In some locations, however, the lighthouse also serves as a Coast Guard station, so personnel are on site at all times.

America's First and Last Official Lighthouse

The Boston Light on Little Brewster Island in Massachusetts (see page 7) was America's very first light station — and it is also America's last, in a way. By 1989, all but one lighthouse in the United States, the Boston Light, had been automated. The automated lighthouses no longer needed lighthouse keepers. Many concerned citizens did not want the same fate to happen to the historic Boston Light — and they took their case all the way to Washington, D.C. They asked the U.S. Congress to please keep the lighthouse manually operated, and the government agreed. For the next several years, the Boston Light was staffed by U.S. Coast Guard personnel, even though the light was eventually automated.

A New Lighthouse Keeper!

In a handmade period costume and with her companion Sammy by her side, keeper Sally Snowman greets visitors to the Boston Light.

Then, in 2003, the Coast Guard decided to once again turn over the reins of the Boston Light to a civilian keeper (not a member of the Coast Guard). A woman named Sally Snowman was chosen to do that job. Sally was not only the first civilian lighthouse keeper appointed since 1941, but she was also the first female lighthouse keeper at the Boston Light.

Today, the Boston Light is the last Coast Guard light station in the U.S. to be staffed with a keeper. You can visit the lighthouse via a boat from Boston. Once on the island, visitors can journey up the 76 stairs to the top! From June to October, National Park rangers are on hand to answer questions and guide visitors around safely.

⟨TRY IT!⟩ E-mail Sally Snowman!

What do you think the life of a modern-day lighthouse keeper is like? Here's your chance to find out! Write an e-mail to Sally Snowman, the current keeper at the Boston Light. Ask her questions about her job and anything else you find curious about living at a lighthouse. Send your e-mail to Sally via the link at www.BostonLight.US.

Holland Harbor Light, Michigan

Thanks to concerned citizens, this lighthouse in Holland, Michigan, is still shining today. In the 1970s, the Coast Guard wanted to deactivate the light. The citizens in the area rallied around the old light station, affectionately called Big Red. Built in 1872, the lighthouse was bought by a historical society and saved. The light still remains lit, and it is maintained by the U.S. Coast Guard.

THINK ABOUT IT!

To date, more than $182,000 has been raised to preserve and maintain the Thomas Point Shoal Light — nearly six times as much as it cost to build the lighthouse!

Do you think it's worth preserving America's lighthouses? What are some of the pros and cons? How might your opinion change if you lived in a different place?

Save Our Lights!

The folks in Berwick, Louisiana, feel so strongly about their lighthouses that they're trying to raise money to move one of them — Ship Shoal Light — to shore and preserve it as a piece of local history. In Maryland, the Thomas Point Shoal Light (page 61) was saved from demolition by a group of citizens who felt very strongly that this historic screw-pile lighthouse deserved to keep its spot in the Chesapeake Bay. The members of the Great Lakes Lighthouse Keepers Association are dedicated to preserving lighthouses in that region, as well as the history of those who tended them.

Even though the age of lighthouses has passed, many people are still lured and fascinated by them. They don't want to see lighthouses fall into disrepair and crumble away. Throughout North America, various organizations are hard at work saving lighthouses that have been deemed no longer necessary. Along with being spectacular to look at, these lighthouses also offer a window to America's past, and this new generation of lighthouse keepers works to preserve this important piece of maritime history. In some cases, efforts are made to keep the lighthouse operational. In other locations, the lighthouse structure is preserved, and if possible, kept open to the public. A tour of a lighthouse can not only show you amazing views, but will guide you through a bygone era before electricity and modern technology were commonplace.

Chatham Light, Massachusetts

Chatham Light sits on the "elbow" of Cape Cod, and it was one of the first lighthouse stations to have not one, but *two*, towers. The government decided to build two lighthouses here to distinguish Chatham Light from another lighthouse nearby. The first pair of towers was built in 1808. Over the years, the lighthouses have been replaced, fortified, and moved. Today, only one tower still stands, but as the ocean constantly reshapes this section of coastline, the remaining light continues to warn mariners of offshore hazards in this area. Members of the Coast Guard live in the station's buildings.

The town of Chatham is still active, too, in preserving the lighthouse. The old lantern and lens of the lighthouse are now an outdoor attraction at the Chatham Historical Society. The land around the lighthouse is eroding, or wearing away. Citizens of Chatham are trying to slow the erosion, but they fear that one day, the lighthouse tower will have to be moved back once again.

TRY IT! Look around for lighthouses!

Although the day of the lighthouse has officially come and gone, people still love lighthouses. If you live or vacation near the coast, visit a local art or photography store and look for paintings or enlarged photographs of lighthouses. Do you recognize any from this book?

Even if you don't live near a coastal area, you might see signs of lighthouses in some pretty unexpected places. Look for lighthouse images:

* on license plates
* as restaurant logos
* as lampposts in people's yards
* on billboards
* as birdhouses
* on stamps

This restaurant sign in Wichita, Kansas, is proof that you just never know where a lighthouse image will turn up!

"Farewell, Tillamook Rock Light Station … long the friend of the tempest tossed mariner. Through howling gale, thick fog and driving rain your beacon has been a star of hope and your foghorn a voice of encouragement … Keepers have come and gone; men lived and died; but you were faithful to the end. Your purpose is now only a symbol, but the lives you have saved and the service you have rendered are worthy of the highest respect."

—final entry in the station log in 1957 by Oswald Allik, the last keeper at Tillamook

Where to Find Them:
A Map of Selected U.S. and Canadian Lighthouses

Grays Harbor
Cape Disappointment
Tillamook Rock

Washington

Oregon

St. George Reef

Point Arena

East Brother
Island

Point Sur

California

Point Vicente

Michigan Island
Grosse Point
Holland Harbor

Waugoshance

Wisconsin

Michigan

Illinois

Indiana

Dunkirk

New York

Pennsylvania

NJ

DEL

Maryland

Virginia

North
Carolina

South
Carolina

Georgia

Alabama

Mississippi

Louisiana

Ship Shoal

Florida

Owls Head
Saddleback Ledge
Maine   Matinicus Rock
               Portland Head
Vermont   Whaleback Ledge
          Cape Ann
NH   Boston
          Minots Ledge
MASS   Duxbury Pier
RI   Chatham
CONN.
               Ida Lewis Rock
Block Island Southeast
Statue of Liberty
Ambrose
Sandy Hook
Navesink
Barnegat
Absecon
Thomas Point Shoal
Portsmouth Lightship
Cape Henry
Bodie Island
Cape Hatteras
Cape Lookout

United States

Ponce de Leon Inlet

Boca Grande

Alligator Reef

Alaska

Cape
Hinchinbrook

The lighthouses labeled in blue are featured
in this book; see INDEX on pages 92 to 93.

Oahu
Makapuu Point

Hawaii

LIGHTHOUSES OF NORTH AMERICA!

Canada

Yukon Territory

Northwest Territories

Nunavut

British Columbia

Alberta

Saskatchewan

Manitoba

Ontario

Quebec

Newfoundland and Labrador

Triple Island

Fisgard

Point Atkinson

Point Clark •

Bois Blanc Island •

Île-Verte

Cap-des-Rosiers
Pointe-au-Père

New Brunswick

Prince Edward Island

Nova Scotia

Miscou Island

Baddeck Harbour
Louisbourg

Sambro Island

Cape Spear
Cape Race
Cape Pine

U.S. Lighthouses Designated as National Historic Landmarks

Block Island Southeast Light, Rhode Island
Boston Light, Massachusetts
Cape Ann Light Station, Massachusetts
Cape Hatteras Light Station, North Carolina
Cape Henry Lighthouse, Virginia
Grosse Point Light Station, Illinois
Navesink Light Station, New Jersey
Ponce de Leon Inlet Light Station, Florida
Sandy Hook Light, New Jersey
Thomas Point Shoal Light Station, Maryland

Canadian Lighthouses on National Historic Sites

Bois Blanc Island Lighthouse, Ontario
Cap-des-Rosiers Lighthouse, Quebec
Cape Pine Lighthouse, Newfoundland and Labrador
Cape Race Lighthouse, Newfoundland and Labrador
Cape Spear Lighthouse, Newfoundland and Labrador
Fisgard Lighthouse, British Columbia
Île-Verte Lighthouse, Quebec
Louisbourg Lighthouse, Nova Scotia
Miscou Island Lighthouse, New Brunswick
Point Atkinson Lighthouse, British Columbia
Point Clark Lighthouse, Ontario
Pointe-au-Père Lighthouse, Quebec
Sambro Island Lighthouse, Nova Scotia
Triple Island Lighthouse, British Columbia

Resources

National Lighthouse Organizations and Web Sites

UNITED STATES

American Lighthouse Foundation
www.lighthousefoundation.org
"Dedicated to saving America's lighthouses and their history"; current lighthouse news and information.

Lighthouse Digest
www.lhdigest.com
This is the online version of *Lighthouse Digest* magazine.

Lighthouse Friends
www.lighthousefriends.com/
Lots of good information, including travel directions and photos.

National Lighthouse Museum
www.lighthousemuseum.org
Great information here. Check out the education programs for quick lighthouse facts.

National Park Service's Maritime Heritage Program
www.cr.nps.gov/maritime/index.htm
Follow the links on this page to: U.S. lighthouses to visit by region; Inventory of Historic Light Stations; list of lighthouses within the National Park System; and the list of lighthouses designated as National Historic Landmarks with links to those lighthouse's sites.

United States Coast Guard
www.uscg.mil/hq/g-cp/history/h_lhindex.html
This site is a treasure trove of lighthouse information. You'll find lists of all existing lighthouses, historical information, and a resource for teachers and kids.

United States Lighthouse Society
www.uslhs.org
This organization sets out to "educate, inform, and entertain those who are interested in America's lighthouses, past and present"; it also offers tours.

CANADA

Parks Canada Agency
National Historic Sites
www.pc.gc.ca/apps/lhn-nhs/index_E.asp
Search under keyword *lighthouse*, and select National Historic Sites only.

3-D Tours
www.pc.gc.ca/apps/dci/source/3d_E.asp
Click on Technology and Engineering for a virtual 3-D tour of five Canadian lighthouses.

Regional Lighthouse Organizations and Websites

UNITED STATES

The Florida Lighthouse Association
www.floridalighthouses.org

Great Lakes Lighthouse Keepers Association
www.gllka.com

Long Island's Lighthouses
www.longislandlighthouses.com

New England Lighthouses
www.lighthouse.cc

New Jersey Lighthouse Society
www.njlhs.org

North Carolina Lighthouses
www.itpi.dpi.state.nc.us/caroclips/homepage.html

United States Lighthouse Society — Chesapeake Chapter
www.cheslights.org

United States Lighthouse Society — Oregon
www.randomb.com/orelighthouse

CANADA

Lighthouses of British Columbia
www.fogwhistle.ca/bclights/index.php

New Brunswick Lighthouses
www.nblighthouses.com

Nova Scotia Lighthouse Preservation Society
www.nslps.com/

LIGHTHOUSE WEBCAMS

Curious about the view from the top of a lighthouse but can't visit one? Check out the websites with the * beside them. Other webcams show the lighthouse itself.

Cape Hatteras Lighthouse Cam
* www.witntv.com/cams/880331.html
www.witntv.com/cams/880286.html

Grand Haven Pier Lights, Michigan
www.lakemichigancam.com

Granite Island Light Station, Michigan
www.graniteisland.com/cam1.shtml

Kincardine Lighthouse, Canada
* www.pilor.com

Portland Head Light, Maine
* www.portlandheadlight.com/webcam.htm

Books

Brown, Jackum. *Lighthouses*. London: Cassell Illustrated, 2005.

Clifford, Mary Louise and J. Candace Clifford. *Women Who Kept the Lights*. Alexandria, VA: Cypress Communications, 2000.

Crompton, Samuel Willard and Michael J. Rhein. *The Ultimate Book of Lighthouses*. San Diego, CA: Thunder Bay Press, 2001.

Holland, F. Ross. *Great American Lighthouses*. New York: John Wiley & Sons, Inc., 1994.

Jones, Ray. *The Lighthouse Encyclopedia*. Guilford, CT: The Globe Pequot Press, 2004.

Rhein, Michael J. *Lighthouse Spotter's Guide*. San Diego, CA: Thunder Bay Press, 2005.

Weintraub, Aileen. *Navesink Twin Lights*. New York: The Rosen Publishing Group's PowerKids Press, 2003. Part of the "Great Lighthouses of North America Series." Other books in the series include: *Alcatraz Island Light, Boston Light, Cape Disappointment Light, Cape Hatteras Light, Point Pinos Light*.

Index

More Good Books from Williamson!

Welcome to Williamson Books! Our titles are available from your bookseller or directly from the Williamson Books website at Ideals Publications. Please see the next page for ordering information or to visit our website. Thank you.

All books are suitable for children ages 7 through 14 and are 96 pages, 10 x 10, $12.95, unless otherwise noted.

Children's Book Council Notable Book
PYRAMIDS!
50 Hands-On Activities to Experience Ancient Egypt

Children's Book Council Notable Book
KNIGHTS & CASTLES
50 Hands-On Activities to Experience the Middle Ages

American Bookseller Pick of the Lists
ANCIENT GREECE!
40 Hands-On Activities to Experience This Wondrous Age

American Bookseller Pick of the Lists
¡MEXICO!
40 Activities to Experience Mexico Past & Present

Parents' Choice Recommended
BRIDGES!
Amazing Structures to Design, Build & Test

Teachers' Choice Award
GEOLOGY ROCKS!
50 Hands-On Activities to Explore the Earth

Benjamin Franklin Silver Award
GOING WEST!
Journey on a Wagon Train to Settle a Frontier Town

Parents' Choice Silver Honor Award
THE LEWIS & CLARK EXPEDITION
Join the Corps of Discovery to Explore Uncharted Territory

Parents' Choice Silver Honor Award
ANCIENT ROME!
Exploring the Culture, People & Ideas of This Powerful Empire

ForeWord Magazine *Book of the Year Finalist*
SKYSCRAPERS!
Super Structures to Design & Build

GARDEN FUN!
Indoors & Out; In Pots & Small Spots
8½ x 11, 64 pages, $10.95

12 EASY KNITTING PROJECTS
8½ x 11, 64 pages, $10.95

40 KNOTS TO KNOW
Hitches, Loops, Bends & Bindings
11 x 8½, 64 pages, $10.95

The following books are suitable for children ages 7 through 14
and are 128 to 160 pages, 11 x 8½ or 8½ x 11, $12.95, unless otherwise noted.

Parents' Choice Recommended
THE KIDS BOOK OF WEATHER FORCASTING
Build a Weather Station, "Read" the Sky & Make Predictions!

Parents' Choice Silver Honor Award
AWESOME OCEAN SCIENCE!
Investigating the Secrets of the Underwater World

Parents' Choice Honor Award
GIZMOS & GADGETS
Creating Science Contraptions that Work (& Knowing Why)

Selection of Book-of-the-Month; Scholastic Book Clubs
KIDS COOK!
Fabulous Food for the Whole Family

Teacher's Choice Director's Choice Award
KIDS' EASY-TO-CREATE WILDLIFE HABITATS
for small spaces in the city, suburbs & countryside

Parents' Choice Recommended Award
WORDPLAY CAFÉ
Cool Codes, Priceless Punzles® & Phantastic Phonetic Phun

GREAT GAMES!
Old & New, Indoor/Outdoor, Travel, Board, Ball & Word

MAKING AMAZING ART!
40 activities using the 7 elements of art design

Parents' Choice Approved Award
THE KIDS' MULTICULTURAL CRAFT BOOK
35 crafts from around the world

Parents' Choice Recommended Award
USING COLOR IN YOUR ART!
Choosing Colors for Impact & Pizzazz

ForeWord Magazine's *Gold Award for Best Children's Nonfiction*
THE SECRET LIFE OF MATH
Discover how (& why) numbers have survived from the cave dwellers to us!

IN THE DAYS OF DINOSAURS
A Rhyming Romp through Dino History
64 pages, 11 x 8 ½, all ages, $9.95

KIDS WRITE!
Fantasy & Sci-Fi, Mystery, Autobiography, Adventure & More!

KIDS CARE!
60 ways to make a difference for people, animals & the environment

THE KID'S GUIDE TO BECOMING THE BEST YOU CAN BE!
Developing 5 traits you need to achieve your personal best

★ ★ ★ **Visit Our Website!** ★ ★ ★
To see what's new at Williamson and learn more about specific books, visit our secure website at:
www.williamsonbooks.com or **www.Idealsbooks.com**

3 Easy Ways to Order Williamson Books:
Please visit our secure website to place your order, or
Toll-free phone orders: 1-800-586-2572
Toll-free fax orders: 1-888-815-2759
All major credit cards accepted
(please include the number and expiration date).

Or, send a check with your order to:
Williamson Books, Orders, 535 Metroplex Drive, Suite 250, Nashville, TN 37211

Please add $4.00 for postage for one book plus $1.00 for each additional book. Satisfaction is guaranteed or full refund without questions or quibbles.